Starting with their gift of a "Little Portion" of their land in Assisi to St. Francis, the Benedictines have always grounded and blessed the Franciscans. I very happily dedicate this book to Fr. John Main, OSB, and Fr. Laurence Freeman, OSB, for giving me—and our world—much more than a little portion of inspiration and encouragement, many spiritual levers, and some very good places to stand. We all thank you!

Dancing
Standing
Still

Healing the World from a Place of Prayer

A New Edition of A *Lever and a Place to Stand*

RICHARD ROHR

With a foreword by James Martin, SJ

Paulist Press
New York / Mahwah, NJ

"The Quickening of St. John the Baptist" (excerpt of 8 lines) by Thomas Merton, from *The Collected Poems of Thomas Merton*, copyright © 1949 by Our Lady of Gethsemani Monastery. Reprinted by permission of New Directions Publishing Corp.

"Humility and Compassion" by St. Francis of Assisi and "The Christ's Breath" by Hafiz. Translated by Daniel Ladinsky, from *Love Poems from God: Twelve Sacred Voices from the East and West*, copyright © 2002, Penguin Compass, New York. Used by permission of the author.

Excerpt from "Dance, Dervish Dance" by Hafiz. Translated by Daniel Ladinsky, from *I Heard God Laughing: Poems of Hope and Joy*, copyright © 2006, Penguin Books, New York. Used by permission of the author.

"I, 4" and "I, 14" by Rainer Maria Rilke. Translated by Anita Barrows and Joanna Macy, from *Rilke's Book of Hours: Love Poems to God*, copyright © 2005, Riverhead Books, New York. Used by permission of the authors.

Except as otherwise noted, the Scripture quotations contained herein are from the New Revised Standard Version: Catholic Edition Copyright © 1989 and 1993, by the Division of Christian Education of the National Council of the Churches of Christ in the United States of America. Used by permission. All rights reserved.

Cover image: *Flowing Rhythm* (in the style of Alexander Calder), by Flensted Mobiles of Denmark. Photograph © Andrew Dunn, andrewdunnphoto.com. Courtesy commons. wikimedia.org.
Cover design by Sharyn Banks
Book design by Lynn Else

Library of Congress Cataloging-in-Publication Data
Rohr, Richard.
    [Lever and a place to stand]
    Dancing standing still : healing the world from a place of prayer : a new edition of A lever and a place to stand / Richard Rohr ; with a foreword by James Martin.
        pages cm
    Rev. ed. of: A lever and a place to stand : the contemplative stance, the active prayer. c2011.
    ISBN 978-0-8091-4867-7 (alk. paper) — ISBN 978-1-58768-357-2
    1. Contemplation. 2. Christian life—Catholic authors. I. Title.
    BV5091.C7R643 2014
    248.3`4—dc23

                                                                2013042421

ISBN 978-0-8091-4867-7 (paperback) / ISBN 978-1-58768-357-2 (e-book)

Published by Paulist Press
997 Macarthur Boulevard
Mahwah, New Jersey 07430

www.paulistpress.com

Printed and bound in the United States of America

Foreword

> God makes us ask ourselves questions most
> often when he intends to resolve them.
>
> — *Thomas Merton*

A few years ago, a friend of mine in Catholic publishing asked if I might like to have dinner with Richard Rohr. It was in the middle of a large religious conference in Los Angeles, where many writers and scholars were speaking to colossal crowds of believers and seekers from across the country. "Are you kidding?" I said, "I'd love to." I had long been an admirer of Father Rohr's extraordinary work and had, just that morning, attended one of his standing-room-only talks. His writings and lectures always — always — remind me of what those who heard Jesus often said about the surprising carpenter from Galilee: "He speaks with authority." Rohr's straightforward approach to the Christian spiritual life is so obviously based in a deeply contemplative stance that his books often surprise people with insights that seem at once completely new and beautifully old — as if he were helping you discover some wonderful truth that you had somehow forgotten.

But then I wondered, "What if he doesn't live up to my expectations?" After all, I had been reading Rohr's works for years and had a well-thumbed and heavily underlined copy of his *Everything Belongs* on my bookshelf. How could the man possibly compete with his books and speeches?

What I didn't understand was that someone who had meditated so deeply on the life of Christ, on the Jewish and Christian scriptures, on the lives of the saints, and, especially, on the story of his beloved St. Francis of Assisi, would be exactly who Richard Rohr turned out to be that night: humble, attentive, insightful, compassionate, and, in a word, alive. What astonished me most about our convivial dinner was how the great man seemed not interested at all in talking about himself, his many books and speaking engagements, or even his marvelous Center for Action and Contemplation. Rather, he was profoundly interested in the Other, or rather the others—the two people with whom he dined that night, much as I imagine Jesus was always lovingly attentive to those with whom he ate, worked, and prayed.

Richard Rohr's book, *Dancing Standing Still*, is, typically, a gem. It is full of the clearheaded and compassionate wisdom that his readers have long expected from this modern spiritual master. The night I met him, Father Rohr surprised me with his humble humanity. May your encounter with him in these pages surprise you with insights and ideas to help you become the person you were meant to be, the person whom God has created.

—Rev. James Martin, SJ, author of
*Becoming Who You Are: Insights on the True
Self from Thomas Merton and Other Saints*

The Greatest Art Form

The Dance of Action and Contemplation

> I die by brightness and the Holy Spirit.
>
> — *Thomas Merton*

I believe that the combination of human action from a contemplative center is the greatest art form. It underlies all those other, more visible art forms that we see in great sculpture, music, writing, painting, and, most especially, in the art form called human character. When action and contemplation are united, we always have beauty, symmetry, and transformation — lives and actions that inherently sparkle and heal, even with dark images.

With most humans, the process begins on the action side; in fact, the entire first half of life for most of us, even introverts, is all about action. We begin with crawling, walking, playing, speaking. We learn, we experiment, we try, we do, we stumble, we fall, we break, and we find. Gradually these enactments grow larger and more "mature," but we remain largely unaware of our inner motivations.

Yes, there are feelings and imaginings during this time, maybe even sustained study, prayer, or disciplined thought, but do not call that contemplation. These reflections are necessarily and almost always self-referential, both for good and for ill. Do not be put off by this; at this point, life is still largely about "me" and finding my own preferred and proper viewing platform. It has to be. But it is not yet the great art form of the union between action and contemplation. We must go further.

The teaching and guidance that is needed is about process more than content. How can I see and use my actions and my reflections to expand and not to contract? How can I listen for God and learn God's voice (which is much more important than knowing God's precise name and plan)? How can I keep my heart, mind, and soul open "in hell"?

> This should be the early form of spiritual
> teaching: not what to see, but how to see.

This should be the early form of spiritual teaching: not what to see, but how to see. I am afraid this cannot usually be taught in book or catechism form; it is picked up largely by "rubbing off" parents and significant others. Could this be the real laying on of hands, the deepest meaning of apostolic succession? Could this be the way the Spirit is passed from vessel to vessel? I think so.

If such soul work is learned, usually by osmosis, we will keep growing—and the contemplative side of the soul will begin to show itself. There are already "hints and guesses," as T. S. Eliot would put it, in the first half of life; and some chosen souls, like Thérèse of Lisieux or Gerard Manley Hopkins, seem to get the hints and make the guesses easily.

For most of us, however, it is a longer process of being drawn by "brightness and the Holy Spirit," as Merton says. Note that Merton says he "dies" by this brightness because, although we are pulled into the Mystery through our actions and beyond our actions in the first half of life, it will be felt and experienced as a kind of dying, a dying into what always feels bigger and brighter.

Contemplation is first of all a series of losses, largely of our illusions. If we did not enter deeply the early learning process of "how," we will use our actions to defend ourselves, protect ourselves from our shadow, and build a leaden manhole cover over our unconscious. We will settle for being right instead of being holy and whole, for saying prayers instead of being one.

The ego wants containment and control. It is only the soul that wants meaning and mystery. In fact, that is how I can know whether it is my ego that is leading me or "brightness and the Holy Spirit"! If I have not found a way to hear and allow that deeper level of soul, I will use all my roles, my relationships, and even my religion to fortify my ego and my private agenda. I might even say a lot of prayers, but it will not be the spacious prayer of contemplation. The "big field" has not yet opened up. The "brightness" has not happened.

Jesus said, "When you pray, do not keep on babbling like pagans" (Matt 6:7; NIV). Contemplation waits for the moments, creates the moments, where all can be a silent prayer. It refuses the very distinction between action and stillness. Contemplation is essentially non-dual consciousness that overcomes the gaps between me and God, outer and inner, either and or, me and you.[1]

The reason why the true contemplative-in-action is still somewhat rare is that most of us, even and most especially in religion, are experts in dualistic thinking. And then we try to use this limited thinking tool for prayer, problems, and relationships. It cannot get us very far. The irony of ego "consciousness" is that it always excludes and eliminates the unconscious—which means it is actually not conscious at all! Ego insists on knowing and being certain; it refuses all unknowing. Most people who think they are fully conscious (read, "smart") have that big leaden manhole cover over their unconscious. It gives them control but seldom compassion or wisdom. That is why politicians, priests, and CEOs will predictably continue to fail and fall as the Inner Mystery shows itself through them and to them.

> We are led forward by brightness, a "larger
> force field" that includes the negative, the
> problematic, the difficult, the unknown...

We are led forward by brightness, a "larger force field" that includes the negative, the problematic, the difficult, the unknown—that which I do not yet understand, the Mysterious that God always Is. Brightness does not exclude or deny anything.

The beauty of the unconscious is that it knows a great deal, whether personal or collective, but it always knows that it does not know, cannot say, dare not try to prove or assert too strongly, because what it does know is that there is always more—and all words will fall short. The contemplative is precisely the person who agrees to live in that kind of brightness. The paradox, of course, is that it does not feel like brightness at all, but what John of the Cross calls a "luminous darkness," and others call "learned ignorance."

In summary, you cannot grow in the great art form, the integrative dance of action and contemplation, without a strong tolerance for ambiguity, an ability to allow, forgive, and contain a certain degree of anxiety, and a willingness to not know—and not even need to know. This is how you allow and encounter Mystery. All else is mere religion.

Of course, you only can do this if Someone Else is holding you in such dying, taking away your fear, doing the knowing, satisfying desire as a great Lover. If you can allow that Someone Else to have their way with you, you will go back to your life of action with new vitality, but it will now be smooth, One Flow. It will be "no longer you" who acts or contemplates, but the Life of One who lives in you (Gal 2:20), now acting for you and with you and as you!

Henceforth, it does not even matter whether you act or contemplate, contemplate or act, because both will be inside the One Flow, which is still and forever loving and healing the world. Christians would call it the very flow of life that is the Trinity. We "live and move and have our being" (Acts 17:28) inside of this one eternal life and love that never stops giving and receiving. This is how you "die by brightness and the Holy Spirit." This is the greatest art form.

Standing Still, Moving Earth

> Give me a lever and a place to stand and I will move the world.
>
> —*Archimedes*

Archimedes (c. 287–c. 212 BC), a Greek philosopher and mathematician, noticed that if a lever was balanced in the correct place, on the correct fulcrum, it could move proportionally much greater weights than the force actually applied. Archimedes imagined a fixed point, the fulcrum, in space. If the Earth rested on one end of a lever, with this fulcrum at this point, and if Archimedes applied his weight on the other side, the force would be magnified by the distance from the fulcrum.

Therefore, if the Earth was distance x from the fixed point, and Archimedes was pulling down on the other end of a lever that was one million times x in length, then his small weight would be magnified a million times and the Earth, theoretically, could be moved. If the lever stretched far enough and the fulcrum point remained fixed close to Earth, even a small weight at one end would be able to move the world at the other.

> The fixed point is our place to stand.
> It is a contemplative stance: steady,
> centered, poised, and rooted.

The fixed point is our place to stand. It is a contemplative stance: steady, centered, poised, and rooted. To be contemplative, we have to have a slight distance from the world—we have to allow time for withdrawal from business as usual, for meditation, for going into what Jesus calls "our private room." However, in order for this not to become escapism, we have to remain quite close to the world at the same time, loving it, feeling its pain and its joy as our pain and our joy. So the fulcrum, that balancing point, must be in the real world.

True contemplation, all the great masters say, is really quite down to earth and practical, and does not require life in a monastery. It is, however, an utterly different way of receiving the moment, and therefore all of life. In order to have the capacity to "move the world," we ironically need some distancing and detachment from the diversionary nature and delusions of mass culture and false self.[2] Contemplation builds on the hard bottom of reality—as it is—without ideology, denial, or fantasy.

St. Francis of Assisi and Thomas Merton continue to have a tremendous impact—even though just single human beings—because their vision was both radically critical of consumer culture and also in love with the world. They overcame the seeming tension and found underneath what I call "the unified field." Thomas Merton called it "a hidden wholeness," and Francis sang of it in his famous "Canticle of the Sun," which has become the de facto theme song of Christian ecology.

Archimedes' discovery is an apt allegory for this tension. Unfortunately, many of us don't have a fixed place to stand, a fulcrum of critical distance, and thus we cannot find our levers, or true "delivery systems," by which to move our world. We do not have the steadiness of spiritual practice to keep our sight keen and alive. Those who have the opportunity for spiritual practice—for example, those in monasteries—often don't have an access point from which to speak to or serve much of our world, beyond religion itself. We need a delivery system in the world with the capacity for building bridges and connecting the dots of life.

Some degree of inner experience is necessary for true spiritual authority, but we need some form of outer validation, too. We need to be taken seriously as competent and committed individuals and not just "inner" people. Could this perhaps be what Jesus means by being both "wise as serpents and innocent as doves" (Matt 10:16)? God offers us quiet, contemplative eyes, but God also calls us to prophetic and critical involvement in the pain and sufferings of our world—both at the same time. This is so obvious in the life and ministry of Jesus that I wonder why it has not been taught as an essential part of Christianity.

> When you are lacking in an experience of
> God, grace, and inner movements of life and
> love, you will lack real spiritual authority.

When you are lacking in an experience of God, grace, and inner movements of life and love, you will lack real spiritual authority. People can tell the difference today. Mere titles or ordination no longer suffice; actual inner experience and authority are what people demand and deserve in our time. Jesus himself was neither a rabbi nor a trained teacher of the law. He was a layman who knew God and God's ways; the twelve that he chose were apparently the same, coming to inner authority through discipleship.

People know when we are just quoting clichés that we hardly believe ourselves, mouthing doctrines that have no real grounding within us, and offering teachings that are mere text-book answers. The innate wisdom of good people is rightly called by the church the *sensus fidelium*, common sense and deep intuition that can taste, smell, and touch the real spirit of God and Jesus (1 John 1:1) and distinguish it from what is bogus or immature. The issues are too global and too urgent today to settle for anything less. As Jesus said in his time, we need "green wood" and not just "dry" (see Luke 23:31). Contemplation, perhaps like nothing else, establishes you inside the *sensus fidelium* of the unified field of the Holy Spirit.

Fortunately, the classic Christian polarities of action and contemplation always feed, regulate, balance, and integrate one another. To even know good, you have to do something first! But then the very limitations and failures of your "doing" will drive you back, and deeper, into contemplation.

And so the cycle of life and prayer begins. After a while you are never sure which is feeding which, or whether it is action or contemplation that comes first. They live through one another, and neither of them can exist by themselves. But finally you will have both your lever and your place to stand—and from there, you can move your bit of the world, because you are being moved yourself inside a Much Larger Flow and Dance.

Putting It Back Together

In his book *Amusing Ourselves to Death: Public Discourse in the Age of Show Business*,[3] Neil Postman argues that modern education, journalism, religion, and almost all public discourse have largely taken the form of entertainment. According to his understanding, Americans are indeed "entertaining themselves to death." Though perhaps not popular, the book has never gone out of print since it was first published in 1985. This is a message we need to hear.

Postman begins the book in this way:

> We were keeping our eye on 1984. The year came and the prophecy didn't. Thoughtful Americans sang softly in praise of themselves. The roots of liberal democracy had held. Wherever else the terror had happened, we, at least, had not been visited by Orwellian nightmares.
>
> But we had forgotten that alongside Orwell's dark vision, there was another—slightly older, slightly less well known, equally chilling: Aldous Huxley's *Brave New World*. Contrary to common belief even among the educated, Huxley and Orwell did not prophesy the same thing. Orwell warns that we will be overcome by an externally imposed oppression. But in Huxley's vision, no Big Brother is required to deprive people of their autonomy, maturity, and history. As he saw it, people will come to love their oppression, to adore the technologies that undo their very capacity to think.
>
> What Orwell feared were those who would ban books. What Huxley feared was that there would be no reason to ban a book, for there would be no one who wanted to read one. Orwell feared those who would deprive us of information. Huxley feared those who would give us so much that we would be reduced to passivity and egoism. Orwell feared that the truth would be concealed from us. Huxley feared the truth would be drowned in a sea of irrelevance. Orwell feared we would become a captive culture.

Huxley feared we would become a trivial culture, preoccupied with some equivalent of the feelies, the orgy porgy, and the centrifugal bumble-poppy [Huxley's names for the drug, sex, and technological diversions in his novel]. As Huxley remarked in *Brave New World Revisited*, the civil libertarians and rationalists who are ever on the alert to oppose tyranny "failed to take into account man's almost infinite appetite for distraction." In *1984*, Huxley added, people are controlled by inflicting pain. In *Brave New World*, they are controlled by inflicting pleasure. In short, Orwell feared that what we hate will ruin us. Huxley feared that what we love will ruin us.[4]

Perhaps Huxley, in fact, was right, and Orwell largely missed the point. This lays a foundation for what I'm trying to affirm in this book: the importance of an inner life, a life grounded in contemplation, a life that searches for the hidden wholeness underneath the passing phenomena, a life that seeks substance instead of simply an endless preoccupation with forms.

The West—and America, in particular—is fascinated with forms. We like impermanent things, maybe because they can't nail us down to anything solid or lasting, and we float in an ephemeral and transient world of argumentative ideas. But this preference isn't bearing substantial fruit. This culture seems to be creating people, especially young people, who are very unsure of themselves, who are grasping in every direction for a momentary sense of identity or importance.

Everything worthwhile puts together
the two things that don't look like they go
together at all, but always have been
connected at a deeper level.

Charles Péguy, the agonized French poet, said with great insight that "everything worthwhile begins in mysticism and ends in politics."[5] Everything worthwhile puts together the two things that don't look like they go together at all, but always have been connected at a deeper level. The goal is to get people to that deeper level, to the unified field, or what I like to call "non-dual thinking," where God alone can hold the contradictions together.

When people ask me which is the more important, action or contemplation, I know it is an impossible question to answer because they are eternally united in one embrace, two sides of one coin. So I say that *action* is not the important word, *contemplation* is not the important word; AND is the important word! How do you put the two together perfectly? I am seventy now and I'm still working on it! It is an art form that will take your entire life to master. To begin with a mystical moment and to end in what looks like politics is the norm, as far as I can see. This is the great dance that we work toward in Christian spirituality.

Unfortunately, too often Christianity has focused on one or the other, but there are some masterful teachers who emphasize the integration of action and contemplation. One of these was John Main; he taught the necessary fixed point, the place to stand, which for him was the stability of the mantra and the disciplined practice of twice-daily formal meditation. And from that daily practice flowed action.

Though he didn't talk directly about social or political issues, Main drew attention to our basic distractions and superficiality. In this he was a prophet, seeing to the depth of things. He spoke from a place of critical distance from the illusions of this world, and in that way his words have weight and substance. His teachings, like that of other great contemplatives, such as Thomas Merton and my father Francis, do have the power to move the world.

There is really only one mystery, one truth,
one suffering, one love, one life, and it is
just showing itself in different forms.

John Main says there is really only one mystery, one truth, one suffering, one love, one life, and it is just showing itself in different forms. He calls it "the universal consciousness of the Risen Christ," which holds this great picture of life together. Augustine called this creative holding of both death and resurrection at the same time "the Paschal Mystery," the place where all transformation happens, the liminal space where God holds paradox.

Moses' experience of the burning bush links action and contemplation. His encounter is surely an inner one, but it is mirrored outwardly as well. It is a transcendent experience, but one that is significantly based in nature and not in a synagogue or temple. Often it is in the open spaces of the natural world that the inner world is most obviously recognized, as the Desert Fathers and Mothers, and Celtic Christianity, remind us. Immediately after Moses has his heart-stopping experience, Yahweh says to him: "I have observed the misery of my people who are in Egypt" (Exod 3:7). God doesn't let Moses float around inside his inner experience. He gives it immediate focus, implication, and direction. And in this case, it is entirely social and political.

The Twelve Steps of Alcoholics Anonymous is another example of authentic spiritual experience, and its connection with the Gospel is profound. Bill Wilson's twelfth step tells alcoholics that they will never really come to appropriate the power and importance of the first eleven steps until and unless they personally take it upon themselves to give it away to at least one other person. This necessary reciprocity is an essential hook from which too many Christians have released themselves and have suffered because of it. I am convinced that, in taking away the need and desire to serve and to pay back, many Christians lose whatever they might have gained in their private devotions.

If I have grown at all in my decades as a priest, it's in part through this role of being a preacher and teacher. I have had to stand before crowds for years and describe what I thought I believed, and then I often had to ask myself, "Do I really believe that myself?" And in my attempt to communicate it, I usually found that I'd only scratched the surface of understanding. In sharing, in giving it away, you really own it for yourself and appreciate more fully its value, beyond what you ever imagined.

This Substantial Mystery is a mystery of participation and never of private ownership.

This Substantial Mystery is a mystery of participation and never of private ownership. Maybe that is why, alongside trying to be faithful to our individual daily prayer, we also commit ourselves to meditating in groups, almost as if to recognize that whatever has happened is not just happening in me, but is happening in us together. The One Spirit is held communally. It is important to experience Spirit in this way, or we can easily become ego-inflated, thinking that "I am so contemplative." The goal is to lessen the fortress of "I," not strengthen the "I" in any apartness or superiority. There is a deep symbiosis in the Body of Christ between the one who thinks he or she is giving and the one who thinks he or she is receiving. The obvious is, very often, completely reversed.

It seems to me that meditation, as John Main taught it, makes it almost inevitable that your politics is going to change, the way you spend your time is going to be called into question, and your snug socioeconomic perspective will be slowly taken away from you. When we meditate consistently, the things that we think of as our necessary ego boundaries—giving us a sense of our independence, autonomy, and private self-importance—fall away, little by little, as unnecessary and even unhelpful. This imperial "I," the self that the West thinks is the only self, is not substantial or lasting at all. It is largely a creation of our own minds. Through contemplation, protecting this relative identity, a persona ("mask"), eventually becomes a trivial concern. "Why would I bother with that?" the True Self asks.

John Main says again and again that it's all about living right here, right now. But, like Eckhart Tolle, John Main reminds us that the mind is incapable of living in the now. The present moment is always boring, and we always hope that the next minute will be better (liberals), or that nostalgia for the past is somehow the truth (conservatives). The mind can do many things, but it cannot be in the present. The mind can rehash the past and worry about the future, or worry about "many things," as Jesus tells Martha (see Luke 10:41), but the mind cannot be present here and now.

The Mystery of Presence

This is why the Doctrine of the Real Presence in the Eucharist is so important. It is the touchstone of orthodoxy, the central sacrament for the journey itself. If we deny that the spiritual can enter the material world, then we are in trouble, since we hope to be just that—spiritual human beings! We had best encounter Incarnation in one focused, dramatic moment, and then the particular truth has a chance of becoming a universal truth. We eat what we are until we know who we are. That is just good nutrition—you become what you eat.

After defending and believing the Real Presence all my life, I recognize that the concept of presence is inherently and necessarily relational. Catholics can defend the Doctrine of the Real Presence all we want, and I do, but if we don't teach the children of God how to be present to presence, there is no Real Presence. We Catholics spend much of our time defending the objective end of doctrines and very often neglect the subjective end—which is where everybody actually lives. Rather than a heady belief—hanging on futile rational arguments about transubstantiation—the Eucharist is about an Encounter of the heart, knowing Presence through our presence. In meditation we move beyond doctrines and dogmas to inner experience.

When we move to the level of experience, we see that this self, which is only a "radio receiver," is not to be taken too seriously, for it is always changing stations and is filled with static and interference. When I am faithful to meditation, I quickly overcome the illusion that my correct thinking, or thinking more about something, can ever get me there. If that were so, every good PhD would be a saint. You see, information is not the same as transformation. Even good and correct thinking is always trapped inside my little mind, my particular culture, my form of education, my parental conditioning—all of which are good and all of which are bad. That places all great mysteries inside my little world, and so we should be much more humble about our own opinions and thoughts. After all, how could the Infinite ever be fully or rightly received by the finite?

> Alongside all our knowing, accompanying
> every bit of our knowing, must be the
> humble "knowing that we do not know."

Alongside all our knowing, accompanying every bit of our knowing, must be the humble "knowing that we do not know."

That's why the great tradition of prayer was balanced by both *cataphatic* knowing, through images and words, and *apophatic* knowing, through silence, beyond words. *Apophatic* knowing is the empty space around the words, allowing God to fill in all the gaps in an "unspeakable" way. This mystical way was almost lost in the West after the dualistic conflicts of the Reformation and the headiness of the Enlightenment. It became unacceptable to have any appreciation for the freedom of not knowing and the spaciousness of not even needing to know!

Strangely enough, this unknowing is a new kind of under-standing. We have a word for it: *faith*, a kind of knowing that doesn't need to know and yet doesn't dismiss knowledge; a kind of knowing that doesn't need to hold everything itself because, at a deeper level, it knows it is being held. As Paul puts it, "For now we see in a mirror, dimly, but then we will see face to face. Now I know only in part; then I will know fully, even as I have been fully known" (1 Cor 13:12).

> This is a contemplative stance toward life,
> our solid place to stand and from
> which to move.

It took me years to understand this, even though this is straight Franciscan teaching; my mind alone could not get me there. Prayer in my later years has become simply letting myself be nakedly known, as I am, in all my ordinariness, face to face, without any masks or religious makeup. Such nakedness is a falling into the unified field, where we know in a different way and from a different Source. This is another access point: know-ing by union, an intuitive grasp of wholeness, a truth beyond words, beyond any need or capacity to prove anything right or wrong. This is a contemplative stance toward life, our solid place to stand and from which to move.

Shadowboxing

There is a deep "okayness" to Life.

When I was a young man, I liked ideas and books quite a lot, and I remember going into bookstores and praying to the Holy Spirit: "Okay, which is the right book that I should read?" Now, when I come back from a longer hermitage retreat, I have no desire to read a book for the next few weeks, or even months. For a while, I know there is nothing in any book that is going to be better, more truthful, or more solid than what I have just experienced on the cellular and soul level. Now, if you asked me what it is that I know, I would be hard pressed to tell you. All I know is that there is a deep "okayness" to Life—despite all the contradictions—which becomes even more evident in the silence. Even when much is terrible, seemingly contradictory, unjust, and inconsistent, somehow sadness and joy are able to coexist at the same time within you. The negative value of things no longer cancels out the positive value, nor does the positive deny the negative.

Whatever your calling, your lever, your
delivery system for the world, it must
proceed from a foundational "yes" to life.

Whatever your calling, your lever, your delivery system for the world, it must proceed from a foundational "yes" to life. Your necessary "no" to injustice and all forms of un-love will actually become even clearer and more urgent in the silence, but now your work has a chance of being God's pure healing instead of your impure anger and agenda. You can feel the difference in people who are working for causes; so many works of social justice have been undone by people who do all the fighting from their small or angry selves. In the stories of Gideon (Judg 7:2–8) and Moses (Exod 14:14), Yahweh had to lessen, or even stop, their compulsive drive so the wind of the Spirit could draw them more gently and more effectively. This is a major and important shift.

Any true contemplation or meditation gradually overcomes your autonomous and success-driven ego. It slowly undoes any illusion that your cracked thinking can get you out of this inexplicable world. It overcomes the shapeless anxiety that comes from the inherent mystery of life and all of your attempts at evasion. That is why your politics, time usage, and economics will change. If they don't, I doubt if your prayer is invading your unconscious. If your prayer goes deep, your whole view of the world will change from fear to connection because you don't live inside your fragile and encapsulated self anymore. In meditation, you are moving from ego consciousness to soul awareness, from being driven to being drawn.

Regardless of our political opinions and values, we must admit that the tenor of public discourse in America is often infantile. Yet many people know of no other way of thinking. No one told them about the wonderful alternative, a third way beyond fight or flight. We have not been offering the Gospel at any depth.

Postman said there are two laws of a culture of entertainment. First, thou shalt have no expectations before or filters afterward. Every television program must be a complete package in itself; no previous knowledge is required. This is an edifice that I can construct, together with the news anchor, in the next thirty minutes, and then come to my own conclusions, although they are usually the news anchor's. No further reading, study, prayer, or conversation is required. I can even put out my own blog, asserting things to be true or false without the least foundation or validation. Precisely because this mode of thinking is so fragile, we wrap ourselves around it very tightly. We have our new cliché, our new opinion, our new conclusion, and that settles all the dust. And we don't like dust; all must be clean, clear, and concluded.

Second, thou shalt induce no perplexity in the discussion. Perplexity is a superhighway to low ratings in America, and that has been statistically proven many times over. A perplexed listener is a listener who will turn to another station. This means that there must be nothing that has to be remembered, studied, applied, endured, or verified. We are willing, like blank slates, to believe the loudest voice, receive the latest poll, take in whatever is being said with conviction and authority. When people have no appropriate filters, culture is susceptible to the whim of demagogues and sound bites. Education should teach us how to create good and helpful filters.

In the Gospel of Luke, when the word *crowd* is used, the crowd is almost always wrong. Mass consciousness, it seems, is never deep or truthful. Mass consciousness cannot hold truth because human truth is always a coincidence of opposites. Take this as normative and even important: any life without conflicts is by necessity only half a life. A certain degree of stress is good and necessary, and shows you are inside of the true Mystery.

> Full human life demands some shadow-
> boxing with the shadow side of every reality.

Full human life demands some shadowboxing with the shadow side of every reality. If we are not willing to do that, if we want the Republicans or the Democrats to be totally right or America to be perfect, then we are incapable of depth or truth. When everything becomes a secure "belonging" system instead of a transformational experience, people simply localize themselves inside their little world of shared beliefs. The fragile self quickly takes on a sense of identity and power: "I'm not very smart myself, but we Catholics as a group are old, big, and right," or "I don't know how we could be oppressing the world. America is always on the side of justice and truth."

So we slide inside our collective identities precisely because we have not found a personal identity, as Paul says, "hidden with Christ in God" (Col 3:3). Before we meet our own soul, most identities are socially mediated. Once we find the inner spring of ourselves and the Holy Spirit, we finally begin to be who we really are. Usually that does not happen until the second half of life, after experiencing failure and loss, but for many, it never occurs.

Remember, every viewpoint is a view from a point. Now, if the point from which I view life is simply my little Richard Rohr self—my American, male, educated, Catholic self—I've got to promote and defend such a little identity. I've got to make sure my viewpoint is the best and always right. Growing up in Kansas gave me quite a strong sense of belonging. I was right in the middle of the good old USA, surrounded with an excess of certitudes about everything. I was not only in the best country in the world, but probably the best state, this side of Oz. And I was "one holy Catholic and apostolic" besides. We were "the one true Church." We were going to heaven. Then we discovered that most other religions believed the same thing.

> There is only one thing more dangerous
> than individual egocentricity and
> that is group egocentricity.

This is called *group narcissism*. There is only one thing more dangerous than individual egocentricity and that is group egocentricity. This happens when the group together agrees upon the same viewpoint, and because the agreement is so total, because no questioning is allowed, it passes for Great Truth. There is great comfort and blindness in such company. The happy Palm Sunday crowd and the angry Good Friday crowd are largely the same people.

This pattern has been around for a long time. Judaism did everything absolutely right and absolutely wrong—just like Catholicism and Protestantism—which we will always do until we experience Substantial Reality. It is religion at the beginning stages, preparing us for Encounter Itself. At the early stage, we fall in love with forms. We promote clichés and external doctrines and dogmas as if they were what Martin Heidegger called "the thing in itself." We do not know the thing in itself yet, so we worship the shell. When we have not experienced the thing in itself, what else can we fall in love with, except forms, flags, boundary markers, and symbols of loyalty? That's what all early-stage religion looks like, swaying "like reeds in the wind," as Jesus would put it. It's not bad; it just means we haven't yet fallen into the hands of a living and loving God.

Until some form of inner journey removes our illusions, the mind will always remain dualistic, eliminating anything problematic or mysterious. Until there is inner experience (which we are calling meditation or contemplation), we can only think in terms of winners and losers. The mind can't even get energy or motivation without comparison: I versus you, us versus them. We try to convince ourselves that we are alive by winning, and we push ourselves to achieve in all kinds of self-created win/lose situations. This is especially the case with men. We get energy as soon as there is a team to beat, a race to run, or an army to fight. Take that away from us and there is a palpable loss of interest in what is happening. If we cannot define a cause in terms of good guys and bad guys, then we actually lose our motivation.

> It is your dualistic mind that will be taken
> from you in meditation, so be forewarned
> if you want to hold on to that.

It is your dualistic mind that will be taken from you in meditation, so be forewarned if you want to hold on to that. Afterward, you will find yourself thinking much more in terms of both/and rather than either/or. This is what enables mystics and saints to forgive, to let go of hurts, to be compassionate, and even to love enemies.

In fact, you cannot do any of the above with a dualistic mind. That's why all great spiritual teachers tell us, in one form or another, "Do not judge" (Matt 7:1). The judging mind is the dualistic mind. It is always comparing and competing. Men tend to compete, women tend to compare, but it is the same ego game. And unfortunately, the comparing and competing soon justify condemning, and then even crucifying, the other. This is the habitual process of the dualistic mind: one side is invariably judged up and the other is invariably judged down.

Soul and Ego

> Can true humility and compassion exist in our
> words and eyes unless we know we too are
> capable of any act?
>
> —*St. Francis of Assisi*

But aren't thought and judgment necessary? Of course they are—at certain levels. It took me a long time to recognize that my need to judge was not really a desire for truth, as I had convinced myself that it was. My need to judge was a desire for control and to be right. That's what is taken away from us in meditation, and that's why many will never go on the inner journey. It gives us some kind of comfort to feel superior and secure; momentary comfort that "I am right" takes away our anxiety. Don't believe me? Watch your own behavior. Control is the first need of the ego. (By the way, if you do not like the psychological term *ego*, I am convinced that Paul is pointing to much the same thing with his word *flesh*, but that word has had an even more unfortunate history, since people thought he meant *embodiment*.)

The ego defines itself by negation and by contraction: "I'm not that. I am not like her. I am not a sinner. I am not a communist. I am not a heretic." When we have not met our True Self, our true identity in God, we are content with what we are not. What we are not demands nothing of us whatsoever except putting someone else down, which is supposed to pull us up! The sad thing is that it works, and so people keep doing it. This won't change unless we find a place to stand, a contemplative stance as the secure True Self. Until then, the False Self will always need to win, be right, and, if possible, defeat the other.[6]

> The soul defines itself by expansion and inclusion—not by saying "no," but by offering a kind of courageous, risky "yes."

The soul defines itself by expansion and inclusion—not by saying "no," but by offering a kind of courageous, risky "yes": "Yes, I am like everybody else, capable of the same good and the same bad. They are all my brothers and sisters." The soul knows that we are all equally naked underneath our clothes. Can you feel the scariness in that? When you allow the face of the other, the opinion of the other, the worldview of the other, to break through your barriers and boundaries, there is always a bit of fear, as in the first moments of intimacy.

I can see why Jesus said, "For the gate is narrow and the road is hard that leads to life, and there are few who find it" (Matt 7:14). He is talking, first, about life in this world. On the unconscious level, I know that true intimacy with anything is going to change me. And if there is one thing that the ego hates more than anything else, it is to change. I know that if I keep doing this meditation, it is going to change my worldview, my priorities, and my preferences. It will be a new world, and I am comfortably hunkered down in this old one. It is a wonder that anyone continues the dangerous journey of prayer, a step-by-step walk into divine and soul intimacy.

Once a radical "justification" (Paul's term for the phenomenon of transformation) has taken place, the self in God is legitimized and we are made one, whole/holy in this world. No wonder it was called "salvation." Then the blind parts of ourselves, the lesser loyalties, take on less and less importance. What meditation does is ground us in a preexistent wholeness that we call Christ Consciousness (1 Cor 2:16), so that we will not identify too much or too long with the mere parts and partialities that make such needless divisions in our world and in ourselves.

If for forty years you have identified with the parts, with the shadow self, the superior self, any passing loyalty system, it's pretty risky to have these taken away from you. If your whole identity is being a Republican or a Democrat, you had better not pray, you really had better not, because your Republican/Democrat identity just isn't going to mean a great deal. Nor will your black/white, gay/straight, rich/poor, American/Asian, or even Christian/non-Christian identity be your rallying cry. You are an utterly new creation, and finally "Christ is all in all" (see Col 3:11, 2 Cor 5:17, and Gal 3:28 if you think this is my idea).

I very much doubt Jesus would salute the United States flag, or any flag of any other piece of God's One Grand Real Estate, which he called the "kingdom of God" or the "reign of God." Do not talk this way, however, in polite religious company, or suddenly you will have "no place to lay your head" and "the whole world will hate you." Why? Because you are not on either side of the usual categories, the usual loyalty systems, and the groups where the ego wants to be to give itself a foundation and a security that it does not actually have. All we can do is go to another place for our foundation and security.

I was teaching in Germany in a Lutheran university during the funeral of Pope John Paul II and the election of Benedict XVI in 2006. The German Lutherans were watching television a great deal then, but I have to admit, I wasn't watching much myself. I wondered why they were so interested.

I have done a lot of work with men's spirituality on what we call the "Father wound" and "Father hunger." The first time I spoke in Germany in the late seventies, my book *Der Wilde Mann (From Wild Man to Wise Man: Reflections on Male Spirituality*, St. Anthony Messenger Press, 2005) had come out, and I went into the Nuremberg Cathedral to talk about it. The cathedral was full to overflowing: men were sitting in the aisles, on the windowsills, and on the floor of the sanctuary. I talked to them for almost an hour on the Father wound.

A young man stood up at the end and said:

> We want to thank you, Father Richard, for coming here. I want to tell you a little about us German people. In the First World War, we killed all of our grandfathers. We were so needy of a father figure, so aimless without a father, that we chose a bad father,

and the rest of the world knows what happened to us
and to you because of that. Now we live in shame as
Germans. Not only did we kill our grandfathers in
the First World War, we then killed all our fathers in
the Second World War.

He choked up and, stretching his arms in both directions,
said, "This cathedral is filled with young men, sons without fathers
and without grandfathers." With the crowd, I was speechless; no
one disagreed or objected to what he said, and many wept.

So in 2006, as I watched the papal funeral and the Germans'
fascination with it, I knew we were not dealing with anything log-
ical. People who were not Catholic and didn't agree with most of
what John Paul II said were also fascinated by him. This was not
reasonable; he served as an "archetypal personality." In a world
that is so incoherent with so much in flux—where there is no
substantial experience of "who I am"—such a need to latch on
to celebrities, strong figures, very often to father figures, becomes,
if not a conscious, then certainly an unconscious and com-
pelling, need. Add to this a mantle of holiness, and many move
toward the father figure like moths toward a flame. But without
healing, we will continue to destroy the world by continued wars,
ecological devastation, and failed relationships at every level.

> Be careful of any "I have" or "I am"
> language, except the great I AM
> that we are in God.

In some circles that I've been in, even contemplation and
meditation have been ways to seek an identity of self-importance.
The disguises of the ego are endless. So we must make sure that,
in taking on a spiritual practice, we are not just seeking moral
high ground in our own eyes, or in the eyes of anybody else. Is

meditation leading me to a new vulnerability and intimacy, or the opposite? Is contemplation leading me to what John Main calls *dispossession*, instead of another new possession? Be careful of any "I have" or "I am" language, except the great I AM that we are in God.

Being Prayed Through

> I am
> a hole in a flute
> that the Christ's breath moves through—
> listen to this
> music.
>
> —*Hafiz*

> God cannot be captured in any form of
> words that we could control or ideas we
> could formulate, but is like the very air,
> breath, spirit in front of our mouth.

A Jewish scientist who was also a rabbi told me something I had never learned in all my studies of the Hebrew Scriptures. He explained that the word *Yahweh*—the sacred Jewish name for God, which we had been told meant I AM—was unutterable and literally unspeakable for the Jewish people. The word *Yahweh* was often substituted with *Adonai* or *Elohim*. In the Hebrew text, the vowels of *Yahweh* are not printed, just the consonants, and readers fill in the vowels with their eyes and mind. That much I knew, but he took it one step further. He pointed out that even the consonants used in the word *Yahweh* are the Hebrew consonants that do not allow us to close our lips or use our tongue. In fact, the sacred name *Yahweh* is an attempt to imitate and replicate the sound of inhalation and exhalation! This is what the great teachers of meditation have always taught us: God cannot be captured in any form of words that we could control or ideas we could formulate, but is like the very air, breath, spirit in front of our mouth.

The word that archetypal religion came up with for God, for the great I AM, was a word mimicking breath itself, unspeakable because it is only breathable. It is the one thing we have been doing since we came out of our mother's body, and the one thing that will only cease when we die and pass into the eternal I AM. Air, breath, wind, and spirit are always beyond us, yet totally around us, within us, and we share in them equally. It is the same air that we all breathe, and yet each of us receives it intimately. No one controls it! It is the utter democratization of religion and offers equal access to the Divine. There is no African or American way to breathe. Hindus and Christians breathe the same air.

I teach this wherever I go, and probably more than anything else, people write back to me that it has changed their entire prayer life and their very capacity for presence to God. Now they pray with conscious loving choice—even while they sleep. Simply inhale, *Yah*, and exhale, *weh*, with mouth open, lips and tongue relaxed.[7]

As John Main says, this is "the poverty of a single word," a word that is hardly a word at all, our very breath. It can't be spoken; it can only be breathed. Though, as we now understand the autonomic nervous system, it is really done to us. We are just the reeds, the instruments, the flutes of God, allowing ourselves to be played.

Silent meditation is the most foundational naming of our

mind problem, offering of an answer, and naming of the mystery within us. There is nothing to possess or claim, just a constant experience of our incapacity to pray at all. Eventually we know that we are being prayed through, and all we can do is allow it, like breathing itself. It is a way to follow Paul's twice-given advice to "pray without ceasing" (1 Thess 5:17). It is the best actual church reform that I can imagine, because it comes from the bottom up and the inside out.

In the "prayer beyond words," which Jesus clearly teaches (see Matt 6:1–6), we move beyond any attachment to, infatuation with, or defense of any single form, and go back to the poverty of a single word and the simplicity of our every breath.

The breath of God

Journey to Spiritual Maturity *To Pg 34*

To continue Archimedes' metaphor of the lever and a place to stand, when we stand with mass culture or cultural Christianity, we have almost no leverage to change the world. I think it is important that we understand how we got into this position, of religion as a belonging system or a mere belief system, and not the radical transformational system—having the mind of Christ—that Jesus intended.

Let me give you a helpful paradigm for understanding our problem. E. F. Schumacher, who wrote *Small is Beautiful*, also wrote a lesser-known book, *Guide for the Perplexed*.[8] Remember, Neil Postman said it's precisely perplexity that we avoid. Schumacher leads us right into seeming perplexity, but then out the other side, too. His explanation is that the three parts of the Hebrew Scriptures—Law, Prophets, and Wisdom—represent the three stages of developing consciousness. Schumacher says that we have to begin our spiritual journey where Jewish revelation begins, and that is with Torah: law, structure, identity, boundaries, certitude, order, authority, and clarity. That is how we can best form a healthy, happy, and secure ego structure.

The alternative to beginning with structure can be disastrous.

The alternative to beginning with structure can be disastrous. The immature ego will arbitrarily pick and choose without any preparation or foundation in any tradition. It is forced to be the center of the world because there is no other center, except freedom to choose, prefer, and decide—moment by moment. This does not help anyone grow up, and when such persons do become adult in age, they tend to feel entitled and poorly prepared for community, friendship, marriage, job, humility, patience, or any kind of union—much less the great divine union.

In short, if we don't begin at stage one with the Law, life gives us tasks we are unprepared for, and inflates the ego far beyond what it deserves. It creates a lethal combination of ignorance and arrogance at the same time, which some say is the very definition of the modern and postmodern self. You and I are not the center of anything, except perhaps our mother's early attention.

Outer authority tells me what the truth is, tells me what to do, tells me what is right and wrong. It's a good and necessary place to start. It's the parent/child relationship that later takes the form of master/pupil and then, if we are lucky, teacher/disciple. Healthy cultures always had elders and traditions so individuals did not have to do everything by themselves—as if we could, anyway. This early need is exactly what we see in books like Exodus, Leviticus, and Numbers: laws, strong boundary-keeping, impulse control, clear group symbols, and the necessity of strict conformity with all of these. This is how religion must begin. It keeps us inside the right boxing ring until we know what the real issues are and what is worth fighting for.

If, however, we stay too long with the first task of life, creating and maintaining our own ego structures, we tend to have a good "container," but we never get beyond the container to the "contents" of life itself. We have learned to rely almost exclusively upon outer authorities that have now become inner conditioning. There must be something more than Law, or we have no need to go on any journey at all, much less a journey of faith.

Most religions stay at this level of Leviticus and Numbers religion, a first half of life religion. It is a good belonging system with clear boundaries and identity. It takes away most self-doubt, and thus people are often quite happy at this stage, if they can succeed at it. It is largely patriarchal, authoritative, top-down religion. After a while, they become so invested in doing the task of Law, and maintaining social and personal order, that they think that is what religion is for! Paul devoted two of his letters, Romans and Galatians, to this problem, and yet we continue to do the same today, as if he did not write them.

Why? I don't think it is bad will on anybody's part. I think it is a lack of contemplative seeing. If we do not go deeper into the mystery of things, religion as container is quite sufficient for most of us. Belonging to groups, feeling the emotion around loyalty symbols, saying "I believe" in this or that, is what the older Catholic tradition once called the first third of the spiritual journey, the "purgative way." It purges us from our basic narcissism and allows us to commit and learn a bit of self-sacrifice, but it is nowhere close to the second and third stages, the illuminative and the truly unitive paths toward God.

There is a second section of the Hebrew Scriptures that we call "The Prophets." Without doubt, this part has been the most ignored, the least quoted, the least influential for Christians, and, I am told, for Jews, too. I suspect this is true because the prophets are always presenting an alternative perspective; they are loyal critics, which is a hard position to hold. They are insiders, but on the edge of the inside. It is not just a rare position to hold, but also to pass on and to legitimate, yet Paul lists it as the second most important role for the building up of the church (1 Cor 12:28). So what happened to it?

Well, no group likes internal critics; they look disloyal and dangerous. No surprise that, according to Jesus, the prophets were all killed (Matt 23:31–32). It is their mystical encounter that gives prophets their authority, and not any ordination or official validation. It is amazing that their books were included in the canonical texts, since they so deeply criticized the secular and religious establishments. The Jewish people are to be credited for institutionalizing this pattern of self-criticism in Scripture. It surely has not been the pattern of Christianity, which has normally excluded most inner critics as heretics, rebels, or unbelievers.

> Once you begin to know for yourself,
> once you've gone deep and have met the
> Holy One, you find that your reliance
> upon outer authority lessens.

Once we move to the prophetic level, stage two, there is an emergence of inner authority. The first level relies almost exclusively on outer authority. Once you begin to know for yourself, once you've gone deep and have met the Holy One, you find that your reliance upon outer authority lessens. You can become rather dangerous at this stage, dualistically switching allegiance totally to your own inner authority. We see it in most teenagers, the rebellion of the 1960s, and the chaos within

much of postmodernism. Many people are so angry and disillu-
sioned with where outer authority has led history, governments,
and churches that they pull all authority inside themselves: "I
won't trust any tradition, any big explanation, anything except
my experiences. I will personally create meaning."

> Jesus represents the mature religious
> position where, finally, we have a person
> dancing between inner and outer authority,
> reaching a new unified field that can
> include both light and darkness.

Schumacher wisely says that the Hebrew Scriptures lead
us to a third, mature stage, symbolized by the Wisdom
Literature, which invariably struggles with paradox and mystery—and leaves us there—while also creating a new but deeper
synthesis. This is especially true in Job, many of the Psalms,
Ecclesiastes, some of Proverbs, and some of Sirach. These writings are not conventional wisdom but alternative wisdom, or, in
our language, contemplative and non-dualistic wisdom. The
Book of Job portrays a psyche finally mature enough to have
faith in the form of darkness instead of light, whereas stage one
insists upon total light and explanation, as we see in fundamen-
talism today. Jesus represents the mature religious position
where, finally, we have a person dancing between inner and
outer authority, reaching a new unified field that can include
both light and darkness.

That is Schumacher's "guide for the perplexed." He says
this third task of living with paradox cannot be tackled until you
have walked the first two. It is a sequential journey. If you stay
in stage one—conformity—or stage two—criticism—you are in
no way ready for mystery, paradox, the collision of opposites that
is the Cross, or, quite simply, you are not ready for adult faith.

You are really not capable of anything except dualistic, either/or thinking.

> At the heart of every mature religion is the same message: you must die before you die.

Further, Schumacher makes it very clear that the movement from stage one to stage two is experienced as a major dying. If you are not trained in dying, you won't go! Most people are not trained in dying, in dispossession, as John Main calls it. To fall back into the Source will first feel more like losing than growing, more like dying than achieving, especially if you have been building and maintaining your personal container for most of your life. At the heart of every mature religion is the same message: you must die before you die.[9]

There is no exception to that in any world religion, yet we prefer to talk about being born again, forgetting that something cannot be born again unless it first dies. Any religion that tells you differently—that it can all be an upward learning curve of success—is lying to you. That is not how transformation happens. This is why there is so little transformative religion; much religion is either a belonging and belief system that asks almost nothing of you, or a reward/punishment system that, of course, doesn't really invite you to fall in love with God at all, but relies upon conformity, along with disguised threat, shame, and fear.

That is what happens when we do not teach people how to pray, which is to move naturally from Law to Prophets to Wisdom: outer authority to inner authority to what Merton calls "the general dance."

Up to now, much of human history has been lived at the first stage of consciousness. It is nobody's fault. We lived to survive and needed to circle the wagons around our own group, national identity, or ethnicity. We needed absolute beliefs, even if they were not always true. So when the floodgates opened on a broad level in the 1960s, many of us tasted the first heady fruits of critical thinking. It was intoxicating, half-true, and dangerous. The immediate results were often impressive. The hippies were my own generation, and we thought that the final stage of enlightenment was achieved in prophetic criticism of the Vietnam War, the legalistic and clerical church, and the racist, classist society. I am now more convinced than ever that it was surely needed. Much of 1950s America and Catholicism was neurotic, prejudiced, smug, and small.

> We can only build on life and what we are
> *for*, not what we are against.

However, everyone gets tired of critique after a while. We cannot build on exclusively negative or critical energy. We can only build on life and what we are *for*, not what we are against. Negativity keeps us in a state of victimhood and/or a state of anger; it's immature if we stall there for long. Mere critique and analysis are not salvation; they are not liberation, nor are they spacious. They are not wonderful at all. We only become enlightened as the ego dies to its pretenses, and we begin to be led by soul and Spirit. That dying is something we are led through by the grace of God and by confronting our own shadow. As we learn to move into a Larger Realm, we will weep over those sins, as we recognize that we are everything that we hate and attack in other people. Then we begin to live the great mystery of compassion that Schumacher calls stage three.

Read to 42

The Wisdom Jesus

In Jesus we have a beautiful symbol of a further stage in human possibility and consciousness. Jesus could clearly deal with opposites and contradictions, and people outside of his own little world. He never taught a reward/punishment system; he never taught a religion. His worldview was much closer to a win/win scenario than the later win/lose game we made it into. If we are honest about our seeming criteria, just about everybody loses and deserves punishment more than reward.

> Most of Jesus' teaching on nonviolence,
> simplicity, downward mobility, forgiveness
> of enemies, and inclusivity has had no
> strong effect on the history of Christianity.

Psychologist Lawrence Kohlberg, in his study of moral development, showed ethical maturity through six levels. He said that we can normally only understand people just one level above ourselves. If you are a person of level-three moral development, with a little stretch, you perhaps can be sympathetic to level-four people—on a good day!

Well, Jesus was a level-six person. If most of religion is happily ensconced at levels two and three, as it seems to be, Jesus and his teaching goes right over most of our heads. "Love those who hate you and persecute you!" We don't get it! Most of Jesus' teaching on nonviolence, simplicity, downward mobility, forgiveness of enemies, and inclusivity has had no strong effect on the history of Christianity, except on those few in every generation and every denomination who undertake the full journey— inner and outer. We must start being honest about this.

So that we can be a little more sympathetic to our history of blatant unfaithfulness to our own Jesus, let me set this in context of scriptural and historical development: why we stalled within Schumacher's first stage of Law and Order. Stage one was firmly established by AD 313, when Constantine made Christianity the official religion of the Roman Empire. To hold an empire together, you need conformity, wars, authority—and you need enemies. Religion was not needed in the West for enlightenment and transformation of persons but to create good citizens for emperor and pope. Christianity was not wanted or allowed as an alternative; it had become the establishment. We literally moved overnight from catacombs to basilicas. We still call our great Catholic Churches *basilicas*—which literally means "palaces," and this is indeed the setting in which we worshipped.

Once Pharaoh is your benefactor and protector, there are many questions you can't ask anymore. You can't ask about liberation of slaves in Pharaoh's house, nor do questions of justice or equality make it to the dining room table. And if you do ask such questions, you will not be answered but quietly—or savagely—eliminated. That was already clear in Exodus. Once we were at the top, we could no longer feel the rejection that Jesus experienced by being born poor in an occupied country. We changed sides, and therefore we changed our point of view: not from the bottom up, but from the top down. The top was where almost all the clergy henceforth resided. That is the perspective for much of our preaching and Scripture interpretation: white, European, educated, comfortable, usually celibate males. I am one myself, and we are not all bad. But we are not *all*.

> For God to be just, therefore,
> is for God to be faithful to God's
> own character and words.

Let's go back to the very concept of God's justice, which begins to be revealed in Torah. If you are God, you don't have any criteria outside yourself that you can conform to and make yourself just. God is simply faithful to who God is. God can only be true to God's own criteria. For God to be just, therefore, is for God to be faithful to God's own character and words. This is very different from any vengeful retaliatory understanding of justice, which is the later juridical understanding. After AD 313, the church criminalized the notion of sin. The church took on the juridical function of the State. However, what God reveals in the Scriptures is that God uses our mistakes to bring us to transformation. Such "restorative justice" is the real and final meaning of biblical justice. God is always using people's mistakes in their favor to transform them. This is what stage-three Wisdom Jesus teaches us.

> God is always using people's mistakes in
> their favor to transform them.

Three Steps Forward, Two Steps Back

This truth about God's character is seen throughout the stories of biblical heroes. Their weaknesses become the means of God's grace. Our capacity for missing the point, however, is understandable because the ego/flesh naturally reads reality as tit for tat, quid pro quo, and reward and punishment. If you do it wrong, you deserve punishment; if you do it right, life rewards you. It's the same story line as in every bad novel. And that's what we have made the Bible into—a bad novel, based on the only story line we are really interested in: where the good guys win and the bad guys lose. It makes sense unless, of course, you are losing, suffering, sinning, or hating yourself. Then you hope for something different. It is to that hope that Jesus came, and to that hope that he most profoundly spoke.

The Bible—reaching its denouement in Jesus—is an alternative reading of history, a "text in travail," as René Girard puts it. The text itself illustrates three stages. Scripture gets the message and holds it now and then, but invariably decides it cannot possibly believe that the good news could be that good, or that God could be that generous, and then it begins to set conditions, prerequisites, and requirements, reverting back to Schumacher's stage one. The entire Bible is always three steps forward, two steps backward; the problem is included in the answer.

> God is the perfect Recycler, and in the
> economy of grace, nothing is wasted.

God's one-of-a-kind job description has God using our problems to lead us to the full answer. God is the perfect Recycler, and in the economy of grace, nothing is wasted. God does not destroy the devil but uses the devil for God's own purposes, which is the ultimate victory, it seems to me.

So God's power for justice is precisely God's power to restore people when they are broken or hurt, and to use their mistakes to liberate them, to soften them, to enlighten them, and to transform them. There is no text in the Old Testament where God's justice is equated with vengeance on the sinner. It might look like it, but if you read the whole paragraph and look at the context, chastisement is always meant to bring us back. God's justice is always saving justice. What is experienced as punishment is always for the sake of restoration, not for vengeance.

Therefore, the justice of the people is to participate in this wholeness and spaciousness of God, to be brought into God's freedom. If we have not mastered nonviolence in Christian countries, is it perhaps because we never nipped vengeance in the bud within ourselves? That is, first of all, the work of prayer. We must face all our demons interiorly, shadowboxing our own illusions, naming, forgiving, and healing our own darkness and brokenness, or we will never know how to do it outside. Take that as a given.

Leviticus—which I referenced earlier as an example of Schumacher's stage-one religion—also holds a capsule of stage-three wisdom (wherein we can't read the Bible dualistically, as either totally perfect or utterly outdated). Americans would probably call the thinking in this passage socialism or even communism: "The land shall not be sold in perpetuity, for the land is mine; with me you are but aliens and tenants….If any of your kin fall into difficulty and become dependent on you, you shall support them; they shall live with you as resident aliens. Do not take interest in advance or otherwise make a profit from them, but fear your God; let them live with you" (Lev 25:23, 35–36).

This rather enlightened text on the sin of usury had significant impact until the twelfth century in the Western Church; it flies in the face of the capitalism that we now take as a given. Until recently, to take interest on a loan when someone was down and out would result in excommunication from the church. Some say that the church never changes, but when we adopt capitalistic thinking, we can drop Scripture and Tradition in a moment. What was once a "mortal sin" is now the name for our Western Christian economies. Capitalism is the making of money from money itself, or "capital," rather than from actual labor, producing goods and services.

> Everything depends upon knowing the
> Holy One, and once you know the Holy
> One, the mystery will flow through you.

Leviticus solidifies its point by grounding the law in the very nature of God: "I am the LORD your God, who brought you out of the land of Egypt, to give you the land of Canaan" (Lev 25:38). In other words, "You got your land free from me, Israel. I own it, so you better give it away freely!" All hinges on that initial God-experience. Now, if you haven't had that initial encounter, you won't understand the law; you won't know how to pass on what you haven't experienced. Everything depends upon knowing the Holy One, and once you know the Holy One, the mystery will flow through you. The Trinitarian dance will begin.

There were ancient Jews in stage three, while many contemporary Christians are happily ensconced in stage one. It all depends on those who "know the Lord, and his ways," those who have an inner life of ego-decreasing, shadow-exposing, glory-revealing prayer. We call it meditation or contemplation, frankly, because the word *prayer* no longer connotes that inner journey for most people. In our practical and utilitarian cultures, prayer became another way to "get" something, when it is much more about "letting go" of something: all the things that we do not need and are not real, anyway.

Jesus affirms, as Living Word, the complete path to maturity, moving from Law to Prophecy to Wisdom. Such wholeness almost inevitably would call forth a whole new religion. Yet there are succinct and wonderful examples of stage-three Wisdom throughout the Bible, so we dare not dualistically and cleanly divide the "Old" from the "New" Testaments. Jesus is simply Judaism at its best and comes fully from that divine matrix. An inner life of meditation or contemplation greases the wheels that move us along the path to Wisdom. Without it, we will always stall at mere Law or criticism.

Economy of Grace

> We must not portray you in king's robes,
> you drifting mist that brought forth the morning.
>
> Once again from the old paintboxes
> we take the same gold for scepter and crown
> that has disguised you through the ages.
>
> Piously we produce our images of you
> till they stand around you like a thousand walls.
> And when our hearts would simply open,
> our fervent hands hide you.
>
> —*Rainer Maria Rilke*

**The key to entering into the
Divine Exchange is never our worthiness
but always God's graciousness.**

The key to entering into the Divine Exchange is never our worthiness but always God's graciousness. Any attempt to measure or increase our worthiness will always fall short, or it will force us into the position of denial and pretense, which produces the constant perception of hypocrisy in religious people.

To switch to an "economy of grace" is very hard for humans. We base almost everything in human culture on achievement, performance, accomplishment, payment, exchange value, or worthiness of some sort—meritocracy. Unless we personally experience a dramatic and personal breaking of the rules of merit, it is almost impossible to disbelieve or operate outside of its rigid logic. This cannot happen theoretically, abstractly, or somehow "out there"!

Our word for that dramatic breaking of the ironclad rule is *grace*. It is God's magnificent jailbreak from our self-made prisons, the only way that God's economy can triumph over our strongly internalized merit-badge system. Grace is the secret key whereby God, the Divine Locksmith for every life and for all of history, sets us free. Life, when lived fully, tends to tool and retool us until we eventually find this key is necessary for our very survival and sanity. Without grace, everything human declines and devolves into smallness, hurt, and blame.

Grace humiliates our attempts at private virtue.

Grace humiliates our attempts at private virtue. Grace makes us feel powerless, poor, empty, and useless. Who wants grace? Only sinners! Only prostitutes, drunkards, and tax collectors, not the proper people. Not the nice or successful people who have no need for any gaps to be filled. They have filled all the gaps themselves.

Perhaps that's why Jesus gave the outrageous, scandalous lesson, "It is easier for a camel to go through the eye of the needle than for someone who is rich to enter the kingdom of God" (Mark 10:25). Now, why didn't we make that rather clear teaching into one of our dogmas or moral mandates? People can't go to communion if they are in a second marriage or openly gay, but they can go to communion all they want if they are multimillionaires—in a world of poor people. You begin to see that we are "cafeteria Christians," picking and choosing what we are ready to hear. If you look closely, you will see that the things we emphasize as truly sinful are usually body-based, and the things we pick as absolutely essential are those that tie us to dependence upon the clergy. Notice how different this selective morality is from the radical morality of Jesus.

Jesus tells his followers, "Set your heart on God's kingdom and God's justice first, and all these other things will be taken care of" (Matt 6:33, my translation). If you are involved in church work, you know that the kiss of death to any lecture series or parish program is to put the word *justice* in the title. You can be assured of a very small attendance, and the program will usually have to be canceled for lack of interest. How did we get to such a place that the things Jesus clearly deemed unimportant—things he never once talked about (for example, birth control, abortion, and homosexuality)—have become the very litmus tests of Christian faith in the last twenty-five years, by people who dare to call themselves traditional or conservative?

The "fundamentals" were quite different in the church's first nineteen hundred years; in fact, they were settled in the early centuries and called the Apostles' Creed and the Nicene Creed. These fundamentals haven't changed. They lack moralism and are much more mystical and cosmological. They place us within a Big Picture, a meta-narrative where we belong and are saved, not by moral perfection or performance, but by God's gracious mercy, inclusion, and initiative.

> Jesus does ask of us strong moral
> decisions, but they mostly have to do
> with changing ourselves, not trying
> to change other people.

Jesus does ask of us strong moral decisions, but they mostly have to do with changing ourselves, not trying to change other people. This one-liner troubled and astonished many, including the disciples who first heard Jesus' words: "None of you can become my disciple if you do not give up all your possessions" (Luke 14:33). To my knowledge, this rather clear passage has not been taken seriously by the papacy, episcopacy, priesthood, or laity. In fact, Christian countries tend to lead the way in the pursuit of luxury and in massive consumption of the goods of this earth. I haven't lived radical poverty myself, either, and I'm supposed to be a Franciscan as well as a Christian.

The only reason I'm daring to say this is because Jesus said it. The man who is often called the "thirteenth would-be apostle," the only one who turned away from a personal invitation by Jesus, is also given a clear prerequisite for following him: "There is still one thing lacking," Jesus tells the rich young man. "Sell all that you own and distribute the money to the poor, and you will have treasure in heaven; then come, follow me" (Luke 18:22). It is astounding that Jesus would dare to name conversion in such a practical and demanding way. Perhaps his answer is hard because the question is egocentric, from a man who is both young and rich. The man's question, "Good Teacher, what must I do to inherit eternal life?" (Luke 18:18) shows no enlightenment or love; it is just glorified and delayed self-interest.

For centuries, we have led people to believe this is the question, but it's just disguised narcissism, religion as an insurance policy, not love of God. Note that Jesus refuses to answer the question directly. He tells the rich boy, in effect, "It is going to take major surgery for you to grow up. Without some clear downward mobility, you will never get it." Passages like this, which ask us to change ourselves, usually are treated as pious nonsense.

Jesus knows that he cannot give this young man another ego possession and let him call it heaven or salvation; the young man has been collecting too long, and it is time for him to pay back. "He became sad, for he was very rich," the story says. Jesus then looked around and said to his disciples, "How hard it is for those who have wealth to enter the kingdom of God!" (Luke 18:23–24). In another place, he tells his disciples explicitly, "You cannot serve both God and wealth" (Luke 16:13). The story continues: "The Pharisees, who were lovers of money, heard all this, and they ridiculed him"—just as perhaps we would. But Jesus goes further: "You are those who justify yourselves in the sight of others, but God knows your hearts; for what is prized by human beings is an abomination in the sight of God" (Luke 16:14–15). Here we see Jesus as an astute psychologist, who recognizes and exposes things that we only now have names for: status seeking, false motives, creation of persona, cultivating a self-image, and denial.

> "I am not here so polite society
> can continue to be polite."

Yet, kindly, Jesus does give us some wiggle room. Toward the beginning of his Sermon on the Mount, he says, "Unless your righteousness exceeds that of the scribes and Pharisees, you will never enter the kingdom of heaven" (Matt 5:20). He is not denying there is a level of virtue or righteousness at stage-one religion. Who wouldn't like a loyal soldier[10] who is on time, clean, and reverent; who salutes you, and does not steal from you? Who wouldn't like it if all in the world showed a sense of basic social order and concern? And yet Jesus says, in effect, "But that's not what I'm here to talk about. I am not here so polite society can continue to be polite."

But that first-stage need is what we have largely made of Jesus' message. Loyal West Point cadets are great for empire building, and on many levels to be admired, but don't equate their work with that of a disciple of Jesus. We have done that, I am afraid, in Catholic schools, religious life, seminaries, and the priesthood. Loyal soldiers will always be canonized; mystics and prophets maybe, but only when we can refashion them into loyal soldiers of the institution. I wonder how you would do that with John the Baptist, or Francis and Clare of Assisi? Their very lifestyles shouted out reform and critical thinking about main-line religion.

Jesus said, "Do not worry about your life, what you will eat, or about your body, what you will wear....It is the nations of the world that strive after all these things....Instead, strive for his kingdom" (Luke 12:22, 30–31). To my knowledge, there is no taboo against five-star restaurants, cosmetic surgery, or fashion design. You would think there might be from the above state-ments. Jesus, by the way, only talks about clothing three times, and in each case, he dismisses its importance or even mocks it. He says it is the pagans who worry about what they are to wear (see Luke 12:30). Another time he makes fun of the clergy, "who like to walk around in long robes" (Mark 12:38). Finally, in his tirade against those who sit on Moses' chair, he points out that they have made the fringes on their clothing long so that others will see them (Matt 23:5). You would think we clergy would go out of our way never to wear any long robe whatso-ever, and certainly not hang tassels at the end of our stoles, which of course is exactly what we do. I do it myself. I love my brown Franciscan habit, but I hope I know I am a Franciscan even when I am not wearing it, and can change if it is going to create a barrier.

> Preoccupation with externals
> corresponds with a lack of deep inner
> experience of the Mystery.

Preoccupation with externals corresponds with a lack of deep inner experience of the Mystery. Once you have touched upon the Absolute, all externals become mere containers, costumes, and signposts, but not even close to the contents. What has to die is not just our self-image but, much more importantly, our attachment to our self-image. Our self-image means nothing to the True Self; it is mere window dressing. But when our windows have too much self-conscious dressing hanging on them, we can't see beyond the windows themselves. Much of "high church" is created by the priests in love with "smells and bells," too preoccupied with the sanctuary instead of the world and the people with whom God is suffering.

Jesus, perhaps disappointingly, gives no abstract theory of social justice. Instead, just as St. Francis does, he makes his life a concrete parable of how to live in this world. He demands of his first followers a living witness to a simple life on the edge, because once you are at the visible center, once you are on the top, you have too much to prove and too much to protect; every great spiritual teacher has warned against it. The only free positions in this world are at the bottom and at the edges of things. Everywhere else, there is too much to maintain—an image to promote and a fear of losing it all—which ends up controlling your whole life. Meditate on Luke 12:22–34, Jesus' sermon about how silly it is to worry, and let it become your worldview, your place to stand. It was my father Francis' favorite passage.

From Poverty to Privilege

Much of what Jesus said seems to have been understood rather clearly during the first several hundred years after his death and resurrection, even taken for granted, before the imperial edict of

313 that pushed us to the top and the center of the Roman Empire. Values like nonparticipation in war, simple living, and love of enemies were common. The *Didache*,[11] written around AD 90, illustrates the commitment to Jesus' teachings. Among many other wise statements, it says, "Share all things with your brother; and do not say that they are your own. If you are sharers in what is imperishable, how much more in things which perish." At this time, Christianity was still pure, simple, and loving, untouched by empire, rationalization, and compromise.

The Shepherd of Hermas,[12] written around AD 120, gives the image of the church as a tower to be built of white round stones, but many stones are not suitable for use in construction. They are not rejected, but they are put away to one side. These stones represent believers who are still relying upon their wealth and success and, therefore, cannot really build this new community. They cannot be used until they have been reshaped and something has been taken from them. That something is their wealth.

Around the year 175, St. Clement of Alexandria wrote a letter entitled "Can a Rich Man Be Saved?"[13] The very fact that it was an active question lets us know that Jesus was still taken seriously. St. Clement, in fact, concludes that it is not necessary to renounce all your worldly possessions to be a believer, but it is surely questionable to be rich.

Tertullian, another father of the church, writes around the year 200, "If anyone is worried by his family possessions, we advise him, as do many biblical texts, to scorn worldly things. There can be no better exhortation to the abandonment of wealth than the example of our Jesus who had no material possessions. He always defended the poor and he always condemned the rich."[14]

The church at this point is a non-imperial church and is still countercultural. How did we lose that free position? After the change of structural position in the year 313, Christianity increasingly accepted, and even defended, the dominant social order, especially concerning war and money. Morality became individualized and largely sexual. It slowly lost its free and alternative vantage point, which is probably why what we now call "religious life" began, and flourished, after 313. People went to the edges of the church and took vows of poverty, living in satellites that became "little churches," without ever formally leaving the big church.

> Standing on the edge of the inside has
> always been a delicate balancing act.

Standing on the edge of the inside has always been a delicate balancing act. I've taken the vow of poverty, for example, but I'm probably more secure today than many, because the Franciscans are going to take care of me until I die and bail me out if I get in trouble. What did the founders of the Franciscan order mean by "vow of poverty"? It was a structural statement about standing outside of the whole world of the market, of production and consumption, of quid pro quo thinking. It was a choice for structural insecurity. Once the climbing "market mind" overtakes the soul, it pretty well destroys any possibility of understanding grace, transformation, and the active power of God. I remember when my novice master told us, almost whispering, "You know we Franciscans are really communists! But don't tell anybody, because that is bad in America."

> Once you are inside, you have
> to defend your power.

If you look at texts in the hundred years preceding 313, it was unthinkable that a Christian would fight in the army. The army was killing Christians; Christians were on the bottom. By the year 400, the entire army had become Christian, and we were now killing the pagans. In a two-hundred-year period, we went from being complete outsiders to directing the inside! Once you are inside, you have to defend your power.

It is during this transition that people like St. John Cassian, Evagrius Ponticus, and the early monks go off to Egypt, Syria, the desert. They are the first group who says, "this self-protective lifestyle is unacceptable." It is in the desert that formal teaching on contemplation was first systematized and taught.

From that point through the modern period, emperors assumed that monks and Christian priests could not fight in war, or kill. Why this split between two brands of Christianity? Even as recently as the Vietnam War, laity could kill, while clergy could not and should not. As a Franciscan, I received an immediate deferment. Is there a connection with our deeper hearing of the Gospel, through the contemplative mind, that does not allow us to kill other people?

Cauldrons of Transformation

I have found that, like almost nothing else, grief brings about transformation if we allow it to teach us. Our usual defenses do not work when we are grieving.

In the men's rites of passage I developed, the men are sent out for an intense "grief day," which has been an essential part of most initiation rites. The grieving mode is an entirely different way of knowing than the fixing, controlling, or understanding mode. In grief work, we know we do not understand, and we never will. We are plunged into unsolvable absurdity and mystery, often with no end in sight. Grief is a portal for many of us, men in particular, into the world of soul and spirit, because it is the first kind of pain or experience that we cannot fix, change, control, understand, or blame anybody for. Not that we won't try! It takes a very great loss, such as the death of someone close to us, to bring us to the deep grief work that moves us to identify with the suffering of humanity, the injustice and absurdity of Earth's pain.

> Through closeness to suffering,
> we are pulled out of our heads
> and into our hearts and sobs.

Through closeness to suffering, we are pulled out of our heads and into our hearts and sobs; we are finally thrown into the belly of the whale, where all transformation and enlightenment happens. Jesus said, "No sign will be given...except the sign of the prophet Jonah" (Matt 12:39). Only exposure to the downside, the shadow self—the "tragic sense of life," as Miguel de Unamuno called it—tends to change people at any depth.

Any overly protected life does not know deeply or broadly. So Jesus did not call us to the poor and to the pain just to be helpful to them, although that is wonderful, too. He called us there for fundamental solidarity with the real and for the transformation of ourselves. We do not go to the edge just to help others, but only after the fact do we realize that it was really to let them help us in ways we never knew we needed. This is a "reverse mission." The ones we think we are saving end up saving us and, in the process, redefine the very meaning of salvation.

Only near the poor, close to the tears of things, in solidarity with suffering, can we understand ourselves, love one another well, imitate Jesus, and live his full Gospel. The view from the top of anything is distorted by misperception, illusions, fear of falling, and a radical disconnection from the heart. You cannot risk climbing there or staying there long. As Thomas Merton said, you spend your whole life climbing the ladder of success, and when you get to the top, you realize it is leaning against the wrong wall.

> I believe that, in the end, there are really
> only two "cauldrons of transformation":
> great love and great suffering.

I believe that, in the end, there are really only two "cauldrons of transformation": great love and great suffering. And they are indeed cauldrons, big stew pots of warming, boiling, mixing, and flavoring! Our lives of contemplation are a gradual, chosen, and eventual free fall into both of these cauldrons. There is no softer or more honest way to say it. Love and suffering are indeed the paths, and contemplative journeys of prayer can keep us on both paths—for the long haul and into deep time.

The Healing Power of Meditation

When religion is not about healing, it really does not have much to offer people in this life. Many have called it "carrot on the stick" theology or, as my friend Brian McLaren says, we made the Gospel largely into "an evacuation plan for the next world." If we don't understand the need and desire for healing, then salvation (*salus* = healing) becomes a matter of hoping for some delayed gratification. We desperately need healing for groups, institutions, marriage, the wounds of war, abuse, race relations, or any of the endless social problems in which we are drowning today. But we won't know how to heal if we never learned the skills at ground zero: the individual human heart.

For much of its history following AD 313, the church's job or concern was not healing, but rather maintaining social and church order: the doling out of graces and indulgences (as if that were possible); granting dispensations, annulments, and absolutions, along with the appropriate penalties; keeping people in first marriages at all costs, instead of seeing marriage itself as an arena for growth, forgiveness, and transformation for wife, husband, children, and the whole extended family; and more. In general, we tried to resolve issues of the soul and the Spirit by juridical means, which seldom works, in my opinion.

Francis MacNutt, the former Dominican who popularized the ministry of healing in the 1970s, wrote *The Nearly Perfect Crime*, a decades-long study of healing in the church.[15] He noted, among many things, that we largely lost the very word *healing* in the mainline Christian churches. It was not even part of our vocabulary until he wrote his first book, *Healing*.[16] The sacrament was called "extreme unction" and, as the name reveals, was put off until the last hours of life. Why not, if the only real goal is the next world? When MacNutt first popularized the notion of healing prayer and healing services, Catholics all thought, "Well, this must come from the Protestants; we are not into healing!" And of course, they were right! Most Catholics didn't expect to really heal people, inner or outer, and as priests, we felt our job was to absolve sin rather than actually transform people. "Get rid of the contaminating element," as it were, rather than "Learn what you can about yourself and God because of this conflict." Those are two very different paths. In the four Gospels, Jesus did two things over and over again: he preached and he healed. We did a lot of preaching, but not too much healing. We did not know how.

I am convinced that if our preaching
does not effect in the listener some level
of healing, then it's not even the Gospel.

I am convinced that if our preaching does not effect in the listener some level of healing, then it's not even the Gospel. Healing is the simplest criterion of preaching the Word that I can imagine. The truth heals and expands you in its very hearing: "the truth will make you free" (John 8:32). It allows and presses you to reconfigure the world with plenty of room for gentleness and peace for yourself, and for those around you. The lived Gospel moves more by inherent attraction than direct promotion. As a preacher for forty years, I know that all we do is get the ball rolling; the preaching itself is not the ball.

Only whole people can imagine or
call forth a more whole world.

If there isn't much correspondence between our religion and our politics, I think it's because we are not involved in the healing of ourselves, so how can we understand the healing of the world? Only whole people can imagine or call forth a more whole world. Healing depends on relating with love and compassion. Official religion usually focuses on imputing and then forgiving guilt. This is much more about sin management than proclaiming a larger-than-life vision for humanity. Remember that the ego contracts around problems. The soul gathers and is drawn by meaning. We clergy settle for the lesser, but more commonly expected, agenda. It really is the best way to keep the laity coming back, strangely enough. I wish it did not work so well.

If we told you about contemplation, where you would know the mercy of God for yourself, you would not be so codependent upon us as clergy. Although this codependency is not engineered maliciously, it creates job security. We all have a hard time doing things that essentially work ourselves out of a job or make ourselves unnecessary. Sin management does hold the flock together, but soon we realize there is little maturity, or even love, in a flock that is so tightly glued. The passive, passive-dependent, and passive-aggressive nature of much of the church is rather obvious.

Our overriding concern has been to help people put up with it, make the best of it, and then, of course, pass on the same kind of oppressive behavior to the next generation, because we have not recognized it as a problem: oppression, persecution, and mean-spiritedness. If we are not about naming and healing such parts of ourselves, how would we possibly know how to transform them in culture, nation state, the military, the earth itself, or even within church institutions? We have a lot of lost time to make up for.

> There is nothing in Jesus' teaching to suggest there should be different levels of discipleship in his vision.

The emergence of the monks, the early Desert Fathers and Mothers, is an unexpected and surprising movement, because there is nothing in Jesus' teaching to suggest there should be different levels of discipleship in his vision. We were all equally called to follow him, but we created our own class system; some people were supposed to "get it" and take it seriously, and some were just along for the ride. The very term layman or laywoman, in any field, applies to people who don't know anything. There are always the professionals and the amateurs. How can that be true if the Gospel hopes to save the world?

> Jesus talked a lot more about praying and healing than anything else.

Could meditation be the very thing that has the power to both democratize and mature Christianity? Meditation alone does not require education, does not need a hierarchy of decision makers, does not argue about gender issues in leadership or liturgy, does not demand licensed officials for sacraments, does not need preachers and bishops, does not have moralistic membership requirements. Meditation lives and thrives with dedicated pray-ers who have every chance of becoming healers in their world, each according to his or her gift. And let's be very honest, Jesus talked a lot more about praying and healing than anything else.

One of Thomas Merton's great complaints was that, as he told his fellow monks (and for which he is still not much loved inside his own monastery), "We are not really contemplatives! We just say a lot of prayers!"[17] That probably came as a shock to the community, and it's a scandal to us: that most religious orders, even those who use the word *contemplative*, were not trained for the most part in the older traditions of wordless prayer or letting go of discursive thought. These people were very often introverted, which is fine, but not, of itself, holy. Prayer beyond words, prayer as a stance, prayer as an alternative consciousness, was rarely taught after the dualistic mind of the Reformation and the rational mind of the Enlightenment nullified the possibility.

From then on, we instead recited prayers and maybe chanted psalms, and filled in the heart gap with lots of pious devotions. That's alright, but it doesn't necessarily take us to that deeper place of the soul; it doesn't deeply touch the unconscious—where almost all our wounds and shadow material are hidden. No wonder prayer did not heal many people, and often religious life was filled with some very neurotic personalities, as we see in the autobiography of Thérèse of Lisieux. The Divine Office, as beautiful as it is, can keep us largely in our heads, our left brains, and our world of good ideas. We can now prove that mere discursive prayer does not access the deeper levels of brain function, but is largely a continuation of our daily, dualistic thought patterns.

A House of Prayer

The cleansing of the Temple—Jesus' central condemning action—can be read on many levels, and it should be. Scholars have come to see that this action is far more important than many of us imagined. It is Jesus' last dramatic, symbolic move before he is killed.

> ### The physical building must be replaced
> ### by the human body of Christ.

The same patterns of meritocracy recur in every age; this will never change until Christianity begins to emphasize a sincere interior life, a world of grace and mercy, as the only antidote when religion has become a worthiness contest. The very architecture and use of the Temple courts make clear how much of a problem this has been, and how the only way out is to make religion "a house of prayer for all the nations" (Mark 11:17), a place where "the blind and the lame" can come to Jesus and be cured (Matt 21:14). Both of these citations come from the story of the Cleansing of the Temple and clearly represent a replacement theology: the buying and selling of God must be replaced by prayer and healing. In John's interpretation, the physical building must be replaced by the human body of Christ (John 2:19–21).

Jesus is saying that the very mentality of the "buying and selling" of God, or love, or mercy, has to go; otherwise religion will always remain corrupt and immature. Love does not happen that way. Yet that is where we went, as predicted by the Temple itself: toward a religion of subtle but real buying and selling, where the clergy became the brokers of worthiness and unworthiness, controlling the membership requirements of who is in and who is out.

This pattern is not unique to Christianity. Hinduism has its caste systems; Buddhism has its upper-class monasteries; Islam is divided both in terms of gender and of office. In Judaism, it is all mapped out in the very architecture of the Temple. What happened to the Temple in Jerusalem is an exact prediction of every religion when it does not go deep but remains concerned with externals, rituals, and boundary markers.

At the physical center of the Temple stood the holy of holies, the place where only the high priest could enter one day a year, the Day of Atonement. Outside the Most Holy Place were the first court of the priests and Levites and the second court for circumcised Jewish men. Then there was the third court, separated by a grate, for Jewish women. Non-Jews, or Gentiles, were forbidden to go beyond the outer or fourth court, under pain of death. Scholars wonder if that is exactly what Jesus is criticizing when he says, "My house shall be called a house of prayer for all the nations" (Mark 11:17).

Do you really think all this division came from God? That God divided Judaism into degrees of worthiness and deliberately separated Jews from the rest of God's people? You would think that monotheists would be the first to move beyond such a mentality.

> Religious marginalization, classism, or
> segregation is especially dangerous
> because it claims to come from God.

If this isn't bad enough, there are seven distinct groups, as declared by the Book of Leviticus, which must remain outside the Temple as impure or "structurally" sinful. That means about 99.9 percent of all the people God ever created are of no serious interest to their Creator. Religious marginalization, classism, or segregation is especially dangerous because it claims to come from God.

The list of the "impure" groups who could not enter any Temple court helps us appreciate the New Testament stories, so I include them here:

1. Those with any kind of contagious or skin disease—lumped under the term *leper* (Any disease that was visible on the outside was deemed to be a punishment from God and a sign of impurity.)
2. The bastard sons and daughters of priests, or anyone born illegitimately
3. People with any visible handicap or disfigurement
4. All women during their menstruation periods and after childbirths
5. Men with injured genitals, most likely including people with ambiguous genitalia, hermaphrodites, and eunuchs
6. Structural, or contextual, "sinners": people whose very occupation put them in touch with dead bodies, unclean animals, or the impure substances listed in Leviticus and Numbers; also all cooperators with Judaism's oppressors, for example, tax collectors; and, practically speaking, anyone who was

presumed not to conform to rules of ritual cleanliness and required temple visits, like shepherds who lived at a distance from synagogue or temple
7. Gentiles—that is, the rest of the world—were variously considered impure, infidels, pagans, lost, and even of the devil

Sinfulness was much more a class, category, state, or occupation than our later notion of internal attitudes and personal malice, which largely comes from Jesus himself! We cannot underestimate how Jesus liberated our idea of what sin might actually be.

Before I get too dismissive of my Jewish friends, remember that I grew up with the Catholic communion rail separating altar boys and clergy (and nuns when they cleaned the altar) from everyone else. The Anglicans solidified this pattern in most English cathedrals, which have altar, sanctuary, clergy seating, boys' choir, choir, and chancel, before we get to the majority of the Christian community. You need a verger to make your way through it all.

It feels clear, clean, and somehow just,
except to people like Jesus.

Nowadays many churches are being built as a circle, providing a more inclusive and inviting sense of community. But it has taken us a long time to get there because we have made religion into a purity contest, and worship spaces usually come to mirror and define that. Once we make the Gospel into a worthiness system, we will create the very things Jesus assaults most in his ministry, but we will also find there something very appealing to the ego, which loves such things. The ego/flesh will create a subtle, or not so subtle, list of what we call debt codes and purity codes to decide who is in and who is out.

These usually have much more to do with cultural fears, biases, and class judgments than anything that actually keeps us from God or leads us to God. But it feels clear, clean, and somehow just, except to people like Jesus.

Jesus turned these debt and purity codes on their heads with his constant touching of and consorting with the impure, the sinners, and the outsiders. It takes downright obstinacy not to see this. Jesus' affirmation of, and choice for, those in the outer courts is in almost every Gospel story. His criticism of the inner court is also clear and even damning. If you can see this, you will never read the Gospels in the same way again, and you will wonder why you did not see it before. It comes down to this, which we can now prove scientifically: people cannot see what they are not told to look for, or to expect. What you decide to see also determines what you do not see. For too long, we've quietly agreed on a common, usually harmless, domesticated interpretation of the Gospels.

> That we could take Jesus of Nazareth and
> make his teaching into a moral matter
> instead of a mystical matter is to miss the
> entire thrust of his reform and invitation.

After you have read the Gospels for a while, you begin to wonder what Jesus did from Sunday to Thursday. He always seems to wait until the period of Friday evening through Saturday evening to do anything. What is wrong with him? Is he lying in a hammock all week? It seems he is intentionally provoking the religious leaders. He goes out of his way to do his big actions on the Sabbath. The Sabbath, along with circumcision and the purity codes, was the primary public boundary marker and loyalty symbol of Judaism in his time. Jesus refuses to be bound by a merely legalistic or ritualistic understanding of his religion. That we could take Jesus of Nazareth and make his teaching into a moral matter instead of a mystical matter is to miss the entire thrust of his reform and invitation. What you decide to look at determines what you do not see.

Creative Questioning   To 7D

As good as charity is, it largely became an avoidance of a basic concern for justice.

The mainline church organized itself around structural charity and almsgiving, but the church lost a deeper sense of solidarity, justice, simplicity, and basic understanding of the poor. No longer were we called to become poor like Christ but simply to help the poor through charity. It became acceptable to get rich personally, even for the clergy, with the idea of passing on that wealth to the poor. But as good as charity is, it largely became an avoidance of a basic concern for justice.

This was certainly a step or two removed from what Jesus lived and invited us into. We are no longer the poor whom Jesus called blessed; from our position of comfort, we take care of the poor. This is good and necessary but not exactly what he taught.

Even though the Catholic Church wasn't a church of the poor, it sometimes became a church for the poor, usually through those specialized groups called religious orders. About two-thirds of Catholic religious orders were founded by wonderful women and men who saw poor boys who were not being taught, poor girls who were not being protected, poor orphans who were not being taken care of. Then one heroic Irish woman would go off and take care of them, and soon we have the Sisters of Mercy, thousands of them.

I'm convinced that, structurally, one of the only reasons Roman Catholicism has lasted is because we have these satellites of freedom on the edge of the inside—the Benedictines, Jesuits, Salesians, and Sisters of Charity and Mercy. They are just doing their job, and every now and then they salute the bishop when he comes by. You can live in our community of Franciscans for six months and not even hear mention of the bishop. I don't mean that disrespectfully; the role is just not that interesting to us. The bishop has questions he is concerned with, and we have different questions, as do most of the laity. Structurally, the church survived because the religious orders and most of the laity just got on with trying to live the Gospel.

> The fruit of meditation is that we ask
> new questions, not in reaction, rebellion,
> or opposition to religion or the church.

The fruit of meditation is that we ask new questions, not in reaction, rebellion, or opposition to religion or the church. We don't have time for that. It's a waste of our life to bother with any kind of oppositional or negative energy, because soon it becomes another form of righteousness, and that would be the death of our contemplative life.

We need to ask questions rather than to have answers; we need to just do the job rather than seek the role and office to do it. Some call this church reformation "Emerging Christianity." We do not react, or leave and form a new group, which would force us into untrue dualistic thinking, wasting time proving the old group was totally wrong and our new group is totally right. We have had five hundred years of this, with an awful lot of bad fruit.

So now we hope to keep one foot in our historic denomination and tradition, grateful for all it gave us, and we put the other foot in prayer groups, service groups, support groups, mission groups, and meditation groups. That is a rather creative, positive, and hopeful way of renewing the church: no longer seeking to be right, but getting down to the practical work of our own transformation and the transformation of our suffering world.

> The best criticism of the bad is
> the practice of the better.

St. Francis knew that he would never reform the church by any frontal, verbal, or theoretical attack. He came, instead, from beneath, from the side—and from the positive. He simply lived in a different and more attractive way. He didn't use oppositional energy. If you go to Assisi today, you can see that Francis went outside the walls, rebuilt little tiny churches, and did it in a way that was beautiful, loving, and positive. The best criticism of the bad is the practice of the better.

Saying Yes

> Why is it much easier for humans to wrap
> themselves around problems, negativity,
> and blaming than around joy?

Perhaps like me, you feel that the longer you live, the more you are forced to ask the question, "What makes people so unkind and hurtful to one another?" What creates mean-spirited people? Sometimes the more petty and unnecessary it is, the more astounding it is. Where does this come from? Why is it much easier for humans to wrap themselves around problems, negativity, and blaming than around joy? It is so strange. Even Peter, entering the tomb on Easter morning, sees, and says nothing (John 20:6–10). His fear overcomes any possible release to joy or hope. The passage ends by saying the disciples went home again, back to their dreariness.

> Maybe we just need to be told how
> deep and hidden the problem is,
> and that there is another way.

You see, humans make hard and impossible the very things we most want. Such contrariness must be the meaning of any original wound or "sin." We really are our own worst enemy. It is not just that we send our unresolved pain and fear toward others, but that we choose to abide in it ourselves. We refuse resurrection on a regular basis and then wonder why we are unhappy. Maybe we just need to be told how deep and hidden the problem is, and that there is another way.

Mean-spiritedness and hate appear to be helpful to us, believe it or not. Negativity works in many immediate and seemingly good ways. It unites a fear-based group far more quickly than love, especially if you do not recognize or admit your own fears. Fear is a well-hidden, denied, and disguised demon. It was the last and latest of the capital sins to be named by the tradition; the Enneagram exposed it as the capital sin of half of the human race![18]

Fear unites the disparate parts of your own False Self very quickly. Remember, the ego moves forward by contraction, self-protection, and refusal, by saying no. Sad to say, contraction gives you focus, purpose, direction, superiority, and a strange kind of security. It takes your aimless anxiety, covers it up, and tries to turn it into purposefulness and urgency, which shows itself in a kind of drivenness. But this drive is not peaceful or happy; it is filled with itself. It is filled with agenda and sees all of its problems as "out there," never "in here."

> The soul, however, does not proceed by contraction but by expansion. It moves forward, not by exclusion, but by inclusion.

The soul, however, does not proceed by contraction but by expansion. It moves forward, not by exclusion, but by inclusion. It sees things deeply and broadly, not by saying no, but by saying yes, at least on some level, to whatever comes its way. Can you feel those two very different movements within yourself? You must not take my word for it; you must see this for yourself and within yourself, or you will never be able to move beyond it.

Just know that Mary's kind of yes (Luke 1:38) does not come easily to us. It always requires that you let down some of your ego boundaries, and none of us likes to do that. What I mean by Mary's kind of yes, as it is presented in the Gospel, is an assent utterly unprepared for, no preconditions of worthiness required, and calmly, wonderfully trustful that someone else is in charge. All she asks is one, simple, clarifying question (Luke 1:34). It is a yes that is pure in motivation, open-ended in intent, and calm in confidence. Only grace can achieve such freedom in the soul, heart, or mind.

When "yes" is asked of us, it will usually be resisted by an attack of anxiety, excuse, or rationalization. We must learn how to recognize our own patterns and the exact shape of our fear. "What is your name?" Jesus asks the Gerasene demoniac (Luke 8:30). We cannot exorcise a demon until we know its exact "name," as it were, and until it shows itself. Pulling the "demon" out of its hiding place in the unconscious, and looking at it consciously and non-defensively, is necessary "shadow work."

It seems that we would sooner have a negative identity than no identity at all.

Contraction allows us to eliminate other people, write them off, exclude them, torture them, and somehow expel them, at least in our minds. This immediately gives us a sense of being in control and having a secure set of boundaries—even holy boundaries, as the Pharisee was seeking when he said, "God, I thank you that I am not like other people: thieves, rogues, adulterers, or even like this tax collector" (Luke 18:11). Hatred or mean-spiritedness gives us a superior sense of identity, even if it is totally untrue, as Jesus says in this story. It seems that we would sooner have a negative identity than no identity at all.

Sometimes it looks like control is behind hatred, but even control freaks are usually afraid of losing something. If we go deeper into ourselves, we will see that there is both a rebel and a dictator in all of us, two different ends of the same spectrum. It is almost always fear that justifies our knee-jerk rebellion or our need to dominate—a fear that is hardly ever recognized as such because we are acting out and trying to control the situation from either the left or the right. Either can be, and often is, a mere ego position. Both positions are afraid of losing their power.

"My deepest me is God!"

Unless there is someone to hold and accompany us on these inner journeys, much of humanity cannot go inside. If only we knew Who we would meet there, and could say, with St. Catherine of Genoa, "My deepest me is God!" Without such accompaniment, most of us will stay on the surface of our own lives; there, mean-spiritedness is the best boundary and protection from being bothered by others. But with such accompaniment, we will literally "find our souls" and the One who lovingly dwells there.

Hatred, however, is a false way of taking away the doubt and free-floating anxiety that comes with the fragility of human existence. Any negative focus takes away existential angst by giving us a false place to stand, but the payoff is that it makes us feel both superior and in control. Hate settles the dust and ambiguity that none of us like. Hate is much more common, I am afraid, and seems much more effective than love. Hate makes the world go round much more than love. Just read the morning paper; the news is largely about who is hating, attacking, accusing, stealing from, or exposing whom. It would not even make news to have a headline saying, "Jane Smith is filled with joy today!" We would not find it interesting and would probably not even believe it.

You could say that Jesus came to reveal and resolve this central and essential problem. I consider it the very meaning of the Risen Christ. There is really no other way to save us from ourselves, and from each other, until we are saved from our need to fear and hate. The pattern is so deep and habitual within humans that we even make religion into a cover for our need to be fearful and hateful.

The ultimate disguise whereby you can remain a mean-spirited person is to do it for God or country. You are relieved of all inner anxiety; you can maintain your positive self-image and even some kind of moral high ground, while underneath are "the bones of the dead," as Jesus said (Matt 23:27). This is what Scott Peck called "people of the lie," from his book of the same title.[19] Scott told me once that he thought this was the most important of his books, but it was one of the weakest in sales. The book hit below the belt; it was too much truth to take.

We have had so much utopian talk about Jesus and love, but Jesus had a very hard time getting to the real issue of love. First, he had to expose and destroy the common phenomenon of fear-hate religion. Once he exposed the lie of hatred and the illusion it created, love could show itself clearly. The pattern is still the same. As Jesus shockingly put it in several places, Satan is the real "ruler of this world" (John 14:30). Hate and fear, it seems, are the ordinary daily agenda.

> Love is the totally enlightened, entirely
> nonsensical way out of this pattern.

Love is the totally enlightened, entirely nonsensical way out of this pattern. Love has to be worked toward, received, and enjoyed, first of all, by facing our capacity for fear and hate. But remember, we gather around the negative space quickly, while we "fall into" love rather slowly, and only with lots of practice at falling.

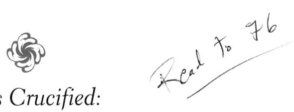

Read to 76

Jesus Crucified: Changing Our Minds

In the thirteenth century, the Franciscans and the Dominicans were the church's debating society, as it were. We were allowed to have minority positions in those days, which makes me think the church has moved backward. We invariably took opposing positions in the great debates in the universities of Paris,

Cologne, and Oxford, and neither opinion was kicked out of the church at that time.

> Jesus is "the image of the invisible God,"
> who came forward in a moment of
> time so we could look upon
> "the One we have pierced" and see
> God's unconditional love.

St. Thomas Aquinas and the Dominicans were being true to the Scriptures, the Jewish temple metaphors of sacrifice, price, and atonement; many passages give you the impression that a ransom is required. But our Franciscan teacher, Blessed John Duns Scotus, who founded the theological chair at Oxford, said that Jesus wasn't solving any problems with God. Jesus wasn't changing God's mind about us, but, rather, he was changing our mind about God. Scotus built his argument much more on Colossians' and Ephesians' understanding of the pre-existent Cosmic Christ. Jesus is "the image of the invisible God," who came forward in a moment of time so we could look upon "the One we have pierced" and see God's unconditional love—and at the same time, what humans do to almost every-thing—and God's unconditional love-response to that.

The image of the Cross was to change us, not to change God, and so Scotus concluded that death was not at all neces-sary: Jesus was a pure gift, and the realm of gift is much better than the realm of necessity. We were not saved because of any problem whatsoever, or to pay any debt to devil or to God, but purely to reveal Divine Love.

The Gospel presents this dilemma in a personal and cathartic narrative that grounds the whole issue in history and in one man's enlightened response to the human pattern. It starts with Jesus accepting the religious and social judgment and hate—"negative unanimity around one," as René Girard calls it: scapegoating. That is why the Gospel emphasizes the role of both church and state—both Caiaphas and Pilate, Jerusalem and Rome—in bringing Jesus to his death. Both major power systems declare him to be unworthy, dangerous, and a sinner.

The One we believe to be the most perfect person who ever lived is judged by power at the highest levels to be, in fact, the problem! The Passion accounts in the New Testament show how wrong power and authority can be. It makes most religious people's love affair with top-down authority rather strange and hard to understand.

Jesus bears the consequences of hatred publicly, but in an utterly new way of forgiveness and letting go, which we finally call "resurrection," not just for him, but for all of history. A new and possible storyline is set forth. Jesus thus transforms the pattern and creates for us the possibility of seeing even the worst things in a new way. He made the worst thing, the "murder of God," into the very best thing, the redemption of the world.

> Jesus was not changing the Father's mind
> about us; he was changing our mind
> about God—and thus about one another.

For two thousand years, Jesus has remained the most striking icon of a possible new agenda. His death exposed the lie and the problem as never before. Jesus was not changing the Father's mind about us; he was changing our mind about God—and thus about one another. If God and Jesus are not hateful, violent, punitive, torturing, or vindictive, then our excuse for the same is forever taken away from us. (Of course, if God is punitive and torturing, then we have full permission to be likewise mean-spirited and negative.)

Jesus' entire journey told people two major things: that life could have a positive story line, and that God was far different and far better than we ever thought. He did not just give us text-book answers from a distance, but personally walked through the process of being both rejected and forgiving, and then said, "Follow me." This is something we can know only by being in that position and coming out even more alive on the other side. It can't be done theoretically or by theological affirmation.

In meditation, we see such things, and weep ahead of time, before we act on them—or let them act on us. That is the message of this book. We need a very "practical practice," or all these words will remain mere interesting ideas that we will soon forget, nor will there be any real transformation of individuals or of our society.

Meditation as Discernment

Paul says, "The angels of darkness must always disguise them-selves as angels of light" (2 Cor 11:15; my translation). For fear to survive, it has to look like reasonableness, prudence, common sense, intelligence; like the need for social order, morality, reli-gion, obedience, or even justice and spirituality. It usually works: just give your fear a nice cover, and you don't have to face that, underneath, you are afraid of losing something. It might take a while to recognize what that something is. This recogni-tion is called the "discernment of spirits" and is listed as one of the major, necessary charisms for the building of the Body of Christ (1 Cor 12:10). It has seldom been seriously taught, except by the Jesuits, because we thought that Law and obedi-ence to Law could resolve all spiritual problems. Someday the church will know that we cannot deal with spiritual things juridically. Paul wrote two letters, Romans and Galatians, addressing this issue, but with little effect on Christian history.

> We need the discernment of spirits to
> know the difference between what is
> apparently or plausibly happening,
> and what is really happening.

We need the discernment of spirits to know the difference between what is apparently or plausibly happening, and what is really happening. It is, indeed, a charism and needs to be compassionately taught. For example, we can call something "justice" while we really mean, and fully intend, vengeance. But the word *justice* sounds good. We hear such misuse of words on the news every night. One wonders if the inner need to punish the other, to hurt the other, has ever been faced, or ever been recognized? When someone has made us afraid, we want to hurt them back, or at least diminish them in some way.

Discernment of spirits is taught and followed by Jesus himself in the telling accounts of his temptations in the desert (Matt 4:1–11). He had to face his own potential for evil, for selfishness, for power, before he could name it or exorcise it in others. If we pretend the demon is not within us, we will never be a good healer or "exorcist." We will almost always project what we refuse to see in ourselves onto others. And please do not call this "mere psychology," for all you need to do is read Jesus' teaching on the splinter in your neighbor's eye and the log in your own, and you will see he is making the exact same point (Matt 7:1–5). Jesus was really quite psychologically sophisticated, or, better, he was in touch with universal wisdom.

*Any contemplative practice is a daily
withdrawing from projections,
denials, and infatuations.*

If you want to see splinters and logs, try sitting, meditating, every morning and every evening for at least twenty minutes. If anybody thinks you are waiting for ecstasy, know that it is invariably twenty minutes of dying! In fact, if you are not learning to let go, but you are still wrapping yourself around your opinions and solidifying your righteousness, then you are not meditating. Any contemplative practice is a daily withdrawing from projections, denials, and infatuations. It is shadowboxing without end, and is nothing less than hard work. As one Buddhist teacher put it, the occasional moment of union or enlightenment is always followed by the ordinary: "After the ecstasy, the laundry!"

To be trapped inside your own small ego is always to be afraid, seeking some kind of control. To not have Someone that you can trust deeply is necessarily to be a control freak. Thus, great religion tries to free individuals from the tyranny of their small and fragile selves and introduce them to Someone-They-Can-Trust. Only if you trust such a Someone will you eventually know that you do not have to create all the patterns and you do not have to solve all the problems. You are being guided.

*Finally you know you are a part
of the general dance.*

You also do not have to explain all the failures, or take responsibility for all the fixing. Finally you know you are a part of the general dance. What else would be the beginnings of peace? As long as you think you've got to fix everything, control everything, explain everything, and understand everything, you will never be a peaceful person. These things largely happen by endless ruminating in the mind. The Enneagram taught many of us that "fear people" are "head people," which was a great surprise to most folks. Our common phrase "peace of mind" is a complete misnomer. When you are in your mind, you are never at peace, and when you are at peace—take note—you are never in your head, but in a much larger, unified field.

Way of the Wound

The process of both denying and projecting your fears and hates elsewhere is called *scapegoating*. The strange word comes from the King James Bible, where instead of speaking of the "escaping goat," they translated it as *scapegoat* (the scapegoat ritual is described in great detail in Leviticus 16). As ritual, it had genius, similar to our ritual of confession today.

On the Day of Atonement, the high priest laid all the sins of the people from the past year on a select goat, and then with reeds the people drove the goat out into the desert. This has become the story line for most of human history. If the problem of ignorant and violent killing is, in fact, the problem at the heart of humanity, you can perhaps see why the "Savior of the World" (John 4:42) would come in this form, revealing both the problem and the correct answer in his final act on Calvary.

> Meditation is refusing to project
> our anxieties elsewhere, and learning
> to hold and face them within
> ourselves and within God.

History up to now has largely been the story of who killed whom and why, and then, afterward, the eventual exposure that the reasons were false or misused. The scapegoat mechanism is hidden in the unconscious; it proceeds from our denied but real need to project our anxiety elsewhere. Unfortunately, there is no elsewhere in the spiritual world. Meditation is refusing to project our anxieties elsewhere, and learning to hold and face them within ourselves and within God.

The very name Satan means the *accuser*. Watch for the accusing spirit within yourself. Notice that, if there is any free-floating anxiety within you, you will always want to think negative thoughts about somebody else. In the spiritual life, we are always our own primary problem. The sign of transformed people is when they can face the often-painful paradox of their existence like Jesus faced it on the cross. I paraphrase Paul: "He became the problem to overcome the problem" (Rom 8:3).

Jesus didn't project the problem on to any other group, race, or religion; he held it and suffered it and thus transformed it into medicine for the world. That is the redemptive pattern, the "third way," or the Paschal Mystery. If you are called to justice work, you cannot begin to do it until you face head-on your own fears, prejudices, and angers concerning these issues. Otherwise, you will be more a part of the problem yourself than a healer for anybody.

The significance of Jesus' wounded body is his deliberate and conscious holding of the pain of the world and refusing to send it elsewhere. The wounds were not necessary to convince God that we were loveable; the wounds are to convince us of the path and the price of transformation. They are what will happen to you if you face and hold sin in compassion instead of projecting it in hatred.

Jesus' wounded body is an icon for what we are all doing to one another and to the world. Jesus' resurrected body is an icon of God's response to our crucifixions. The two images contain the whole message of the Gospel.

> ## We come to God not through our strength but through our weakness.

Jesus agrees to be the Wounded One, and we Christians are these strange believers in a wounded healer. If I were to name the Christian religion, I would probably call it "The Way of the Wound." We come to God not through our strength but through our weakness. We learn wisdom and come to God not by doing it all right but through doing it all wrong. Our Jesus is a victim before he is a victor and, on some level, we are, too.

If you were going to create a religion, would you think of creating, as your religious image, a naked, bleeding, wounded man? It is the most unlikely image for God, the most illogical image for Omnipotence. None of us in our wildest imagination would have come up with it. It must expose a central problem, for God to come into the world in this form and in this way. We Christians have now become accustomed to it—perhaps we have domesticated it—and we no longer receive the shock and the scandal of all that it is saying.

> ## The cross of Jesus was a mirror held up to history, so we could spot and stop the pattern.

Scapegoating works so well that there is no likely reason to think it is going to end or change. Until we are enlightened by grace, we don't even see it; it remains safely hidden in the unconscious where it plays itself out. A Gospel passage describes this unconscious pattern: "When the unclean spirit has gone out of a person, it wanders…looking for a resting place, but it finds none. Then it says, 'I will return to my house from which I came'" (Matt 12:43–44). Rather than have our self-doubt or self-hatred come home to roost, we make sure it finds a resting place somewhere else. Once we spot and stop the pattern, the game is over. The cross of Jesus was a mirror held up to history, so we could spot and stop the pattern.

Only the great self, the True Self, the Godself, can carry such anxiety. The little self can't do it. People who don't pray can't live the Gospel because the self is not strong enough to hold the anxiety and the fear. If we do not transform our pain, we will always transmit it. Always someone else has to suffer because we don't know how to suffer; that's what it comes down to. Watch for any spirit of accusation; as soon as it comes, mistrust it; usually you are running from yourself.

Some have said that the best we have been able to do in the last forty years is to move hatred to ever higher forms of sophistication and ever more subtle forms of disguise, but we still love to hate: feminists can hate men, liberals can hate conservatives, socialists can hate rich people, good family-values folk can hate homosexuals, and victims can hate perpetrators.

Most people are like electric wires: what comes in is what goes out. Someone calls us a name, and we call them a name back. That is, most people pass on the same energy that is given to them. Now compare an electric wire to those big, ugly, grey transformers that you see on telephone poles. Dangerous current or voltage comes in, but something happens inside that grey box and what comes out is, in fact, now helpful and productive.

That is what Jesus did: he hung on the cross and did not return the negative energy directed at him. He held it inside and made it into something much better. He is our new and pure electric current. He is not paying any price to God, as if God needed to be talked into loving God's creation. Jesus is paying a price to the soul—so that we can see! That is how "he took away the sin of the world." He refused to pass it on! Until the world understands that, there will be no new world.

Finding Our Charism

Night is our diocese and silence is our ministry
Poverty our charity and helplessness our tongue-
tied sermon.
Beyond the scope of sight and sound we dwell
upon the air
Seeking the world's gain in an unthinkable
experience.
We are exiles in the far end of solitude, living as
listeners
With hearts attending to the skies we cannot
understand:
Waiting upon the first far drums of Christ the
Conqueror,
Planted like sentinels upon the world's frontier.

—*Thomas Merton*

**To meditate daily is to have chosen,
accepted, and surrendered to a vocation.**

When I read this passage from Merton's poem, "The Quickening of St. John the Baptist,"[20] I think of meditators. I think of what Christian contemplatives have taken upon themselves, "planted like sentinels upon the world's frontier," doing something that, frankly and unfortunately, will never fill stadiums. To meditate daily is to have chosen, accepted, and surrendered to a vocation. We must think of it that way. It is a vocation that places us at the center of history and yet also at its very edge, because most will see us as innocuous, pious, or maybe even self-centered. That poverty might well be our deepest charity, Merton seems to say. Most people won't know that we are holding it all together, that we are the miniscule moment that somehow hears, re-creates, allows, and passes on "the first far drums of Christ the Conqueror."

> We are holding it all together...
> we are the miniscule moment.

I have tried to talk about the place to stand; about the True Self, the integrated self; about the big vision, the big picture that we try to hold together. But I haven't talked much about the lever. Maybe I have hesitated to do that because I don't believe there is just one lever; I believe there are many. As Paul so beautifully says, placing all our gifts inside of one great Trinitarian flow: "Now there are varieties of gifts, but the same Spirit; and there are varieties of services, but the same Lord; and there are varieties of activities, but it is the same God who activates all of them in everyone" (1 Cor 12:4–6). Paul sees us together as a fourth presence of the Holy Trinity, invited into the Divine Dance.[21]

> It seems to me that much of the
> proper work of the church should
> be the discerning and empowering
> of gifts for the world.

It seems to me that much of the proper work of the church should be the discerning and empowering of gifts for the world. There doesn't seem to be much discernment, even in seminaries, as to whether one really has a gift of Christian leadership, reconciling, healing, preaching, or counseling. These free gifts—as opposed to offices, roles, or something for which one is merely educated—are true charisms.

Most of us who are ordained had to discover if we actually had any charisms only after we were ordained. How strange and painful for those who were not gifted in preaching, and yet had to stand up and preach, week after week; or for those who had no gift for wisdom or counseling or healing, and yet had people put their lives trustfully in their hands. Untold damage has been done because we let office, role, title, vestment, and formal ordination substitute for the free gifts of God. It is almost as if we could not trust that such gifts could or would be given.

> It takes being "swallowed by a beast"
> and taken into a dark place of nesting and
> nourishing that allows you to move to a
> deeper place called personal vocation.

I am convinced that the Book of Jonah can best be read as God moving someone from a mere sense of religious job or career to an actual sense of personal call, vocation, destiny, or delivery system. It takes being "swallowed by a beast" and taken into a dark place of nesting and nourishing that allows you to move to a deeper place called personal vocation. It involves a movement from being ego-driven to being soul-drawn. The energy is very different. It comes quietly and generously from within you, and you do not look for payment, reward, or advancement because you have found your soul gift.

I have met many people who have found their soul gift, and they are always a joy to work with. You can tell they are not counting the cost, but just want to serve and help. Benedictines have a group that they call *oblates*, which means "those who are offered." To come with your life as an offering is quite different from the seeking of a career, security, status, or title. Even the Vatican Office for Bishops dared to admit publicly that they were worried about the rampant careerism among bishops worldwide: the seeking of promotion to higher and more prestigious dioceses. It sounds like we still have James and John wanting to sit at the right and left sides of the throne of Jesus. Maybe the young man or woman needs to start there, but you see why Jonah has to be shoved out of the boat, or he will never get to the "right" Nineveh.

> Meditation should lead to a clarity about
> what you are and, maybe even more,
> what you are not.

Listen, wait, and pray for your charism. Most of us are really only good at one or two things. Meditation should lead to a clarity about what you are and, maybe even more, what you are not. This second revelation is just as important as the first. I have found it difficult over the years to sit down and tell people what is not their gift; it is usually very humiliating for the person to face their own illusions and sense of entitlement. We are not usually a truth-speaking people; we don't speak the truth to one another, nor does our culture encourage the journey toward the True Self. The false self often sets itself up for unnecessary failures and humiliations. Just watch the auditions for the television show *American Idol*. That so much certainty of a talent can coexist with so much lack of any actual talent really defies analysis. One wonders if these people have any truly loving friends who would tell them the truth. But if it is true in the church, it is because it is true in the whole culture.

Three Ways to Help

I think there are three basic levels of social ministry, and none is better than the other. First, imagine a river flooding out of control—symbolizing the circumstances and injustices that bring about suffering—overflowing its banks and sweeping those in its path off their feet.

At the first level, we pick drowning people out of the swollen river, dealing with the immediate social problem right in front of us: a man comes to our door and says he is hungry, and we give him a sandwich, or even invite him inside. These are hands-on, social service ministries, like the proverbial soup kitchen. Such works will always look rather generous, Christian, charitable, and tend to be admired, if not always imitated. This first level does not take a lot of formal education, usually just a big heart, and a ready gift of time or money.

Second, there are ministries that help people not to fall into the swollen river in the first place, show them how to survive despite falling in, or teach them to understand how the river flows. In general, these are the ministries of education and healing. Most of the religious orders in the Catholic Church in the last three hundred years went in that direction. That is why we have filled our country with schools, hospitals, and social service ministries, whereby we could help people who were going to fall into the swollen river, give them the skills so they wouldn't fall in, or show them survival skills if they ever did. These ministries empower people and give them new visions and possibilities for their own lives, and for their own dignity.

Finally, some ministries build and maintain the dam that

will stop the river from flooding in the first place. This is the work of social advocacy and activism, critique of systems, organizing, speeches, boycotts, protest, and resistance against all forms of organized injustice and deceit. This kind of ministry surely demands the highest level of education, perseverance, and courage (because we usually fail to achieve our goal). We have to know how to access the system, how the system works, and how to speak the language and understand the maneuvers of those on the inside. Most of us don't have the self-confidence or background that is needed to do this difficult work! It is the gift of a few, but a much needed gift, and largely only emerged after the 1960s, as we began to understand the real meaning of the prophetic charism and call.

> Do one or two things wholeheartedly in
> your life: that is all God expects and all
> you can probably do well.

I don't think most people feel called to activism; I myself don't. Several times in Washington, I was arrested and led off in my Franciscan habit. I was making my statement, and hopefully supporting others; but I had to finally say that it was not what I was called to do. It was humiliating to admit, and I lost the trust and admiration of some friends and supporters. But as we come to know our soul gift more clearly, we almost always have to let go of some other "gifts" so we can do our one or two things with integrity, instead of always being driven by what has been called "the tyranny of the urgent." Soon urgency is a way of life, and things are not done contemplatively or peacefully from within. Do one or two things wholeheartedly in your life: that is all God expects and all you can probably do well. Too much good work becomes a violence to yourself and, finally, to those around you.

A Generative Life

The important thing is that we all should be doing something for the rest of the world. We have to pay back, particularly those of us born into privilege and comfort. We also must respect and support the other two levels, even if we cannot do them. Avoid all comparisons about better or lesser, more committed or less committed; those are all ego games.

> When justice work is not charity,
> then it is not true justice.

Let's just use our different gifts to create a unity in the work of service (Eph 4:12), and back one another up, without criticism or competition. Only in our peaceful, mutual honoring do we show forth the glory of God. When justice work is not charity, then it is not true justice. And when charity work does not promote justice, it is not, finally, charity.

The Gospel is not about being nice; it is about being honest and just, and the world doesn't like those two things very much. Our job is to learn how to be honest, but with love and respect. Martin Luther King, Jr., taught us that before you go out to witness for justice, you have to make sure in your heart that you can love and respect those who disagree with you.

Can you image the surrender necessary for those who have been oppressed for generations? Frankly, I don't know how you can do it without meditation. How could you go to that deep place where you do not want to publicly expose, humiliate, or defeat your opponents, but rather work, as King said, for win-win situations? Seeking win-win solutions, not win-lose, takes a high level of spiritual development and demands spiritual conversion.

When you are hurt, you want to hurt back; when you are put down, you want to put down the opponent. I've met so many wonderful social activists. I often agree with their conclusions and with their politics, but, to be honest, I am often disappointed in their actual energy, goals, and seeming motivation. They seem to be as alienated, angry, and negative as are the people on the other side of the argument.

> They start being drawn instead
> of being driven.

You change sides from inside—from the power position to the position of vulnerability and solidarity, which gradually changes everything. Once you are freed from your paranoia, from the narcissism that thinks you are the center of the world or from your belief that your rights and dignity have to be defended before other people's rights and dignity, you can finally live and act with justice and truth. Once these blocks are taken away from you—and that is what contemplative prayer does—then you just have to offer a few guiding statements of social analysis and people get it for themselves. They start being drawn instead of being driven.

True contemplation is the most subversive of activities because it undercuts the one thing that normally refuses to give way—our natural individualism and narcissism. We all move toward the ego, and we even solidify it as we get older if something doesn't expose it for the lie that it is—not because it is bad, but because it thinks it is the whole and only thing! People don't really change by themselves; God changes us, if we can expose ourselves to God at a deep level. This is why Christian meditation will never fill stadiums; not so many people want their narcissism and separateness to be exposed for the silliness that it is.

Eric Erickson, in his analysis of the stages of men's growth (it applies to women, too), said that if a man doesn't become generative somewhere between the ages of fifty and sixty-five—meaning someone who generates life for the next generation and not just for himself—then he enters into what Erickson called "estrangement." He is foundationally estranged from himself and the rest of the world as he tries to secure his last twenty years around himself. No one ever told him there was anything more than building his own tower.

Perhaps our own fathers and mothers thought that the final stage of life was about taking care of themselves, and we know we do not want to go in that direction. How could a culture with so much education, so much opportunity, and so much supposed enlightenment, produce so many people who become so petty in their final years? I think they never became generative people because they never heard the Gospel, much less how to internalize it. Will believers be in any position to lead the way and set the tone? I hope our prayer practice is preparing us for real servant leadership, the kind that Jesus so clearly taught (Luke 22:24–27) and modeled (John 13:12–15).

Journey of Descent

I have found the phenomenon of male initiation in every culture and on every continent, until the modern era.[22] Something that universal—and so uniform in its goals—was surely fulfilling a deep human and social need. It was deemed necessary for cultural survival, it seems. Initiation might be called "religion before the great world religions began" and, interestingly enough, it was only the male who had to be taught. Women learned in other ways. It is the oldest form of spiritual instruction in the world that we know of.

We recognize in initiation universal patterns of wisdom that need to be taught to the young male or else he becomes useless, dangerous, and a loose cannon in the social fabric. The male seeks his own power, his own advancement, and his own career to the neglect of just about everybody else. The male is very inclined, it seems, to narcissism, and this has to be exposed, humbled, and used for good purposes.

> Worship of Jesus is rather harmless
> and risk-free; following Jesus
> would change everything.

In the early stages of a young man's "tower building," initiation teaches him about a necessary downward journey. The major principle is this: if the male is not led into journeys of powerlessness, we can assume that he will use, misuse, and abuse his own power in his own favor. This pattern seems clear in the history of the church and modern societies. Jesus clearly taught the twelve disciples about surrender, the necessity of suffering, humility, servant leadership, and nonviolence. He was initiating them! The men resist him every time, and so he finally has to make the journey himself and tell them, "Follow me!" But we avoided that, too, by making the message into something he never said: "Worship me." Worship of Jesus is rather harmless and risk-free; following Jesus would change everything.

Lenin is supposed to have said, shortly before he died, that if he had to do his Russian revolution over again, he would ask for ten Francises of Assisi instead of more Bolsheviks. He had realized that something imposed by domination, power, and enforcement from above only creates the same mirrored response on the other side. He realized that the only "communism" that would ever be helpful to the world was the voluntary and joyous simplicity of a Francis of Assisi.

That clear message of Jesus' teaching has not been taught with any great seriousness in the church. It was never expected of the clergy—certainly not of the higher clergy—and, therefore, why would we ask it of the rest of the church? Jesus was training the leaders, because they could only ask of others what they themselves had done first. Once we saw the clerical state as a place of advancement instead of downward mobility, once ordination was not a form of initiation but a continuation of patriarchal patterns, the authentic preaching of the Gospel became the exception rather than the norm—whether Orthodox, Catholic, or Protestant.

I have often thought that this "non-preaching" of the Gospel was like a social contract, as we shake hands across the sanctuary. We agree not to tell you anything that would make you uncomfortable, and you will keep coming to our services. It is a nice deal, because once the true Gospel is preached, I doubt if churches would be filled. But the discernment and the call to a life of service, to a life that gives itself away instead of simply protecting and procuring for itself in the name of Jesus, is what parishes could and should be about.

Making Friends in the Middle

When we look at history, we can see a constant swinging back and forth between two poles, representing two necessary values. Those values have something to do with the first task of life and the second task of life, but they also need one another.

The first value seeks order, certitude, and control, and it is the best way to begin. But what eventually emerges is a critical alternative consciousness. Whenever Law and Order is overdone, another group of people reacts against it. Once there is an establishment, there will eventually be a disestablishment. When some have all the power, those who don't have power ask very different questions, and the pendulum swings back again—eventually. That has been the story of most of history and the sequencing of most revolutions. It is understandable and predictable, although the extremism on both sides could be avoided if we had more initiated elders who held the middle.

We took the idioms *Right* and *Left* from the Estates General in France, where to the right of the throne sat the nobility and the clergy, and on the left sat the commoners—90 percent of the population. Those terms are now commonly used in the political world. The Right is normally concerned with status quo, stability, continuity, and authority; that is a legitimate need. Without it, we have chaos; we don't know our place to stand. Those on the Right are normally considered innocent until proven guilty. Those on the Left are presumed to be guilty until proven innocent.

But some form of the Right is necessary
for authority and continuity in a culture,
and some form of the Left is necessary
for truth and reform in a culture.

The powers that be have tended to write history from the side of the victors. Once you see this, you wonder why you never saw it before. But some form of the Right is necessary for authority and continuity in a culture, and some form of the Left is necessary for truth and reform in a culture. Thus, the pendulum swings, and we all hope we are living at the time when it is swinging toward our side!

In the biblical tradition, these two poles are symbolized by the kings and the prophets. There is a necessary opposition between them. There is only one instance in the Hebrew Scriptures that those two ever make friends, and then only barely. This is when David the King accepts the critique of Nathan the Prophet, after Nathan accuses him of his sinfulness and David has the humility to admit, "I have sinned against the Lord" (see 2 Sam 12).

The Right considers itself the product of rationality, experience, and civilization. The Left is just "silly" people's movements arising out of high-minded ideology, unbearable injustices, or both. The Left's movements are not rational or well planned at the beginning; they are intuitive and come from the suffering of the little people, who are of no account and have no press or status. Thus, they rely on symbols, songs, slogans, and charismatic leaders to get off the ground. The biblical pattern of Exodus has been repeated time and again. Martin Luther King, Jr., showed all the marks of a biblical prophet, even to the final prediction of his death. He knew where that kind of truth was going to lead him.

The Bible is a most extraordinary text
because it repeatedly legitimizes, not the
people on the top, but invariably the
people on the bottom.

Most of political and church history has been controlled
and written by people on the Right because they are educated.
One of the few subversive texts in history, believe it or not, is
the Bible. The Bible is a most extraordinary text because it
repeatedly legitimizes, not the people on the top, but invariably
the people on the bottom. The rejected son, the barren woman,
the sinner, is always the chosen one of God! We see their helplessness—and what marvelous symbols of powerlessness they
are—and then, out of that powerlessness, God creates power.

It is like the necessary first step of the Twelve Steps—the
realization that we are powerless; then, through our eleventh
step of "prayer and meditation," we find our Higher Power. If we
don't walk through that clarification and conversion, it doesn't
happen.

Typically, institutional theology is the legitimation of what
we are already doing and what we need to be true. For example,
at the Council of Trent in 1545, we said that there are seven
sacraments, there always were, and there always will be. That is
patently not true, but had become the Catholic practice at that
time. We couldn't back down in the presence of Martin Luther,
so we falsely asserted that we always believed it and that it was
always that way. In fact, there were only two sacraments for
much of our history: baptism and Eucharist.

The history of the sacraments is itself a pendulum swing
between the needs of the Left (the laity) and the demands of the
Right (the clergy). If the needs of the Left actually won out, I
suspect we would have seventy sacraments instead of seven: the
washing of feet, forgiveness ceremonies for failed marriages,

communal prayer over the sick, liturgies of lament, agape meals, public reconciliation rituals, cleansing of warriors after war, and so on.

It took until the second half of the twentieth century for the Left to have a public and legitimate voice outside the Bible itself. In any swing of the pendulum in the direction of justice, the masses, the bottom, were always considered subversive and traitorous, until the last century. And it's easy to see why, when even the church was looking down from the top and the Bible had been made into establishment literature. The Bible clearly affirms law, authority, and tradition, as most writings in most of history have done, but then it does something further and even stronger: it affirms reform, change, and the voiceless. This is what makes the Bible an inspired book.

> The Bible is biased; it takes the side of the rejected, the poor, the abandoned, the barren women, and those who have been excluded, tortured, and kept outside.

That bias toward the bottom, assumed in the Bible, has now been adopted in the new constitutions of much of the world's religious orders. Religious life is an alternative consciousness. The bias has been called by some "the preferential option for the poor." It is an *option*, an *invitation*; it is a grace, and it emerges from inner freedom—or else it would not be from God. Nevertheless, it is clearly the chosen option of the Bible. In other words, the Bible is biased; it takes the side of the rejected, the poor, the abandoned, the barren women, and those who have been excluded, tortured, and kept outside.

The Perfect Medicine

You see, I want a lot.
Maybe I want it all:
the darkness of each endless fall,
the shimmering light of each ascent.

So many are alive who don't seem to care.
Casual, easy, they move in the world
as though untouched.

But you take pleasure in the faces
of those who know they thirst.
You cherish those
who grip you for survival.

You are not dead yet, it's not too late
to open your depths by plunging into them
and drink in the life
that reveals itself quietly there.

—*Rainer Maria Rilke*

You have to die before you die,
and then you know.

Why does the Bible, and why does Jesus, tell us to care for the poor and the outsider? Because we need to stand in that position for our own conversion. We need to understand the mercy of God, the forgiveness of God, the grace of God. We have to stand under the waterfall so we need it, yearn for it. When we are too smug and content, then grace and mercy have no meaning.

Forgiveness is not even desired. When we have pulled ourselves up by our own bootstraps, religion is always corrupted because it doesn't understand the Mystery of how divine life is transferred, how people change, how life flows, how we become something more and fall into the great compassion. It has been said that religion is largely filled with people who are afraid of hell, and spirituality is for people who have gone through hell. As all initiation rites say: you have to die before you die, and then you know.

Jesus is always on the side of the crucified ones. He changes sides in the twinkling of an eye to go wherever the pain is. He is not loyal to one religion, to this or that group, or to the worthy; Jesus is always loyal to suffering. Do you realize that takes away all of our usual places to stand? In other words, he is just as loyal to the suffering of Iraqi boys as he is to the suffering of American boys. He grabs all our boundaries away from us, and suddenly we are universal people.

> God is on the side of pain,
> wherever the pain is.

God is on the side of pain, wherever the pain is. God is on the side of all human suffering. Try to preempt Jesus now for your own group, religion, or country. It is impossible. Jesus is what mythology called a "shape-shifter," and no one seeking power can use him for their private purposes. Those whose hearts are opened to human pain will see Jesus everywhere, and their old dualistic minds will serve them less and less, for the Shape-Shifter ends up shifting our very shape, too.

The only and simple prerequisite for the touch and healing of Jesus is desire itself. The only people who want God's healing are those who have longed for it, whose hearts have been emptied out by suffering and pain. They call out, like the blind man on the road, "Jesus, Son of God, have mercy on me," and Jesus moves right toward him, as he does with all who ask.

A lawyer who joined our Franciscan Province said to me one day, "You know, this church is harder and harder for me to understand. You claim to have the perfect medicine, the healing power to restore and renew hearts and souls, but you also always seem to be saying, 'Make sure you don't really need it, because if you really need it, you are a less than ideal member!' Forgiveness, reconciliation, compassion, and healing are mere concessions to the unfortunate instead of the very path of salvation itself. But in fact, they are the very nature of God."

> In the Eucharist, we move beyond
> mere words and go to that place where
> we don't talk about the mystery anymore;
> we begin to chew on it.

In the Eucharist, we move beyond mere words and go to that place where we don't talk about the mystery anymore; we begin to chew on it. We move our knowing to the bodily, emotional, and cellular level. I think that it is easier for God to convince bread of what it is than to convince people. It's easier for God to convince wine; wine will have no problem knowing that it is the Blood of Christ, but we do. So clergy keep feeding us the medicine. We keep drinking and eating the mystery until one day it will dawn on our deepest soul, "My God, I am what I eat!"

Meditation shows us the same thing as Eucharist. After twenty-five minutes of meditating, we can believe what has been true since the first moment of our existence: that we are the very Body of Christ. We have dignity and power flowing through us that we have not earned; it has been totally given to us as a gift from God.

Eckhart Tolle says, in his book *The Power of Now*, that 83

percent of human thought is repetitive and useless. I wrote to him and said I only disagree with him in one aspect: I don't think it is 83 percent; I think it is 93 percent. We really do think we are our thinking. We get obsessed with these patterns of thought and, I'm convinced, as we get older, it gets more difficult.

Scientists are now saying that the neural grooves that we prefer, and use repeatedly, become ingrained patterns in the brain. If we cease thinking alternatively, then alternative ways of thinking die. And so the neural grooves that we prefer to use take over by the time we're in our forties and fifties, and that is probably why a lot of old people are not very interesting; they have four or five remaining neural grooves, and we know what they are going to say before they say it. There is no originality, no freshness or immediacy of response, and therefore there is no seeing.

> Contemplation is trying to address
> the root, the underlying place, where
> illusion and ego are generated.

Christians who meditate are self-initiating people, and since we no longer have formal rites of passage in our cultures, we need contemplation to change us. Faithfulness to contemplative practice can achieve the same radical inner renewal as sacraments and formal initiation rites. Contemplation is trying to address the root, the underlying place, where illusion and ego are generated. It touches the unconscious, where most of our wounds and need for healing lie. With meditation or contemplation, I think we have every likelihood of producing actual elders for the next generation, and not just elderly people.

Dancing in the Unified Field

Dance, dervish, dance—
Bring the Face of God before you.

Only Love can lift the heart up so high
That its true Color is restored by the Sun!
See Him near and clapping,
That Perfect One who fathers Divine Rhythm.

....

O dance, Hafiz, dance.
Write a thousand luminous secrets
Upon the wall of Existence
So that even a blind man will know
Where we are,
And join us in this Love!

—Hafiz

Hope, it seems to me, is the fruit of a learned capacity to suffer wisely and generously. The ego needs success to thrive; the soul needs only meaning. The Gospel gives our suffering personal and cosmic meaning, by connecting our pain to the pain of others and, finally, by connecting us to the very pain of God. Any form of contemplation is a gradual sinking into this fullness, or what I have been calling here the unified field, which always produces a deep, irrational, and yet certain hope.

People of such prayer are doing themselves a great favor, or, as Jesus says, they get a hundred times more in this life, which bubbles forth into a limitless life, and eternal life later (Matt 19:29). If we have it now, we will have it then. Why would God not give divine union to us later, while giving it so freely, gratuitously, and undeservedly now? Why would God change the policy? A life of inner union, a contemplative life, is simply practicing for heaven now. God allows us to bring "on earth as it is in heaven" (Matt 6:10) every time we allow, receive, and forgive the conflicts of the moment and sit in peace and freedom. God holds together all the seeming opposites and contradictions.

> Contemplation is no fantasy, make-believe,
> or daydream, but the flowering of
> patience and steady perseverance.

Contemplation is no fantasy, make-believe, or daydream, but the flowering of patience and steady perseverance. When we look at the world today, we may well ask whether it can be transformed on the global level. There is a deep relationship between the inner revolution of prayer and the transformation of social structures and social consciousness. The Book of Wisdom says "the multitude of the wise is the salvation of the world" (Wis 6:24). Our hope lies in the fact that meditation is going to change the society that we live in, just as it has changed us. It is that kind of long-term thinking that God seems to be involved in and kindly invites us into the same patient process.

I know the situation in the world can seem dark today. We see theological regression into fundamentalist religion, which thinks that all issues can be resolved by an appeal to authority (either hierarchy or Scripture), and so it has no need for an inner life of prayer. It desperately doubts and fears inner authority, which, as we said, is the new covenant that Jesus and

Jeremiah promised us. In America, we have seen the rolling back of a compassionate economic system and the abandonment of our biblical responsibility for the poor. Fear and anger seem to rule our politics and our churches. We see these same things in many other parts of the world.

The negative forces are very strong, and the progressive development of consciousness and love sometimes feels very weak. But a Great Turning is indeed happening, as people like Joanna Macy, David Korten, and Thomas Berry believe and describe.

In his Letter to the Romans, Paul has a marvelous line: "Where sin increased, grace abounded all the more" (Rom 5:20). In so many places, there are signs of the Holy Spirit working at all levels of society. The church might well have done its work as leaven, which both Jesus and Paul speak of, because much of this reform, enlightenment, compassion, and healing is outside the bounds of organized religion. Only God is going to get the credit.

> We are the people resulting from the
> Word that became flesh and continuing,
> ever deeper, embodiment.

Take, for example, the word *nonviolence*. It didn't exist in the English or German languages in the year 1900 because the concept didn't exist. Jesus lived a nonviolent life, taught it, and died it, and the tradition that proceeded from his teaching didn't even understand the concept enough to have a word for it. Now consciousness and awareness have evolved so that we can talk about such things. Justice and healing have only become common words in the last century. Once there is the word, there are the beginnings of consciousness. And we are the people resulting from the Word that became flesh and continuing, ever deeper, embodiment.

The toothpaste is out of the tube. There are enough people who know the big picture of Jesus' thrilling and alluring vision of the reign of God that this Great Turning cannot be stopped. There are enough people going on solid inner journeys that it is not merely ideological or theoretical. For the first time, on a broad basis, this reformation can come from the inside, and in a positive, nonviolent way. This reformation is not just from the top down, but much more from the bottom up. Not from the outside in, but from the inside out. Not from clergy to laity, but from a unified field where such class questions are of minor importance. The big questions are being answered at a peaceful and foundational level, with no need to oppose, or deny, or reject. I sense the urgency of the Holy Spirit, with seven billion humans now on the planet at the same time. There is so much to love and embrace.

That, to me, is a significant breakthrough in our very understanding of the character of a reformation. Contemplatives are on the front line of such a reform. Groups like Contemplative Outreach and the World Community for Christian Meditation are, prophetically, ecumenical. I am convinced that the only future of the church, the one Body of Christ, is ecumenical and shared. Each of our traditions have preserved and fostered one or another jewel in the huge crown that is the Cosmic Christ; only together can we make up the unity of the Spirit, as we learn to defer to one another out of love. In contemplative prayer, so many of our historical, ritual, and language differences are of little importance now.

If it seems to you that I have been overly hard on Catholicism, Christianity, organized religion, or even my country of the United States of America, I want to point out that it was these very institutions that gave me the criteria, and held me inside the crucible long enough, to come back and critique Christian America by its own stated values. If I had not butted up against the church's inconsistencies, and my own inconsistencies, I don't think I would know anything. If I had just wandered around inside my own head, outside of some good containment and guidance from both Scripture and Tradition, I would not dare to speak; I would lack the spiritual discipline to move beyond the surface.

> Spiritual progress, ironically, develops
> through tragedy and through falling.

So it seems to me that true progress, or the hope that we have, is not naïvely optimistic, a straight line, or without regression. Spiritual progress, ironically, develops through tragedy and through falling, where we end up, as C. G. Jung said, "finding pure gold," the gold of the Gospels, and, most surprisingly of all, the hidden gold of our own souls, and the soul of the world.

You might even say, at this point, that our "place to stand" becomes our best and biggest "lever" to move the world. Our free fall into Pure Be-ing becomes our very best do-ing.

Notes

1. Richard Rohr, *The Naked Now: Learning to See As the Mystics See* (Chestnut Ridge, NY: Crossroad, 2008).

2. Richard Rohr, *True Self/False Self* (Cincinnati, OH: St. Anthony Messenger Press, 2000). CD.

3. Neil Postman, *Amusing Ourselves to Death: Public Discourse in the Age of Show Business* (New York: Penguin Books, 1985).

4. Ibid., vii–viii.

5. Marjorie Howard Villiers, *Charles Péguy: A Study in Integrity* (New York: Harper, 1965).

6. Richard Rohr, *Immortal Diamond: The Search for Our True Self* (San Francisco: Jossey-Bass, 2013).

7. Rohr, *The Naked Now*, 25–26.

8. E. F. Schumacher, *A Guide for the Perplexed* (New York: Harper Perennial, 1978).

9. Richard Rohr, *Adam's Return: The Five Promises of Male Initiation* (Chestnut Ridge, NY: Crossroad, 2004).

10. Richard Rohr, *Discharging Your "Loyal Soldier": Moving Beyond Early Religious Conditioning* (Albuquerque, NM: Center for Action and Contemplation, 2009). DVD.

11. Tony Jones, *The Teaching of the Twelve: Believing & Practicing the Primitive Christianity of the Ancient Didache Community* (Brewster, MA: Paraclete Press, 2009).

12. Carolyn Osiek and Helmut Koester, *The Shepherd of Hermas (Hermeneia: A Critical & Historical Commentary on the Bible)* (Minneapolis, MN: Fortress Press, 1999).

13. *Clement of Alexandria: The Exhortation to the Greeks. The Rich Man's Salvation. To the Newly Baptized* (fragment) (Cambridge, MA: Harvard University Press, Loeb Classical Library, 1919).

14. Tertullian, "The Apology," *The Ante-Nicene Fathers* (Peabody, MA: Hendrickson Publishing, 1995).

15. Francis MacNutt, *The Nearly Perfect Crime: How the Church Almost Killed the Ministry of Healing* (Ada, MI: Chosen, Baker Publishing Group, 2005).

16. Francis MacNutt, *Healing: The Most Comprehensive Book Ever Written on Healing through Prayer* (New York: Bantam Books, 1980).

17. Rohr, *The Naked Now*.

18. Don Richard Riso and Russ Hudson, *The Wisdom of the Enneagram* (New York: Bantam, 1999).

19. M. Scott Peck, *People of the Lie: The Hope for Healing Human Evil* (New York: Touchstone, 1998).

20. Our Lady of Gethsemani Monastery, *The Collected Poems of Thomas Merton* (New York: New Directions, 1977).

21. Richard Rohr, *The Divine Dance: Exploring the Mystery of Trinity* (Albuquerque, NM: Center for Action and Contemplation, 2004). CD. Richard Rohr and Cynthia Bourgeault, *The Shape of God: Deepening the Mystery of Trinity* (Albuquerque, NM: Center for Action and Contemplation, 2004). CD.

22. Rohr, *Adam's Return*.

CENTER FOR ACTION AND CONTEMPLATION

Center for Action and Contemplation (CAC) is home to the Rohr Institute, an educational center grounded in the Christian mystical tradition. Founded by Richard Rohr, OFM, in 1987, CAC has a growing, international reach, touching lives regardless of denomination, religion, or culture. CAC encourages the transformation of human consciousness through contemplation and seeks to equip and empower people to live out their sacred soul tasks in service to the world. Fr. Richard's teachings form the basis of the nonprofit's vision and ongoing work.

CAC is located in Albuquerque, New Mexico, but many of its programs and resources can be accessed from anywhere in the world. Educational offerings include daily meditations (free e-mails sent every day), self-paced online courses, Living School (two-year program combining onsite and online learning), Conspire Symposia (annual events in New Mexico), online bookstore (comprehensive selection of Fr. Richard's books and recordings), and publications such as the journal *Oneing*. Learn more at cac.org.

ABOUT THE AUTHOR

Fr. Richard Rohr is a globally recognized ecumenical teacher, bearing witness to the universal awakening within Christian mysticism and the Perennial Tradition. He is a Franciscan priest of the New Mexico Province and founder of the Center for Action and Contemplation (CAC) in Albuquerque, New Mexico. Fr. Richard's teaching is grounded in the Franciscan alternative orthodoxy—practices of contemplation and lived kenosis (self-emptying), expressing itself in radical compassion, particularly for the socially marginalized.

Fr. Richard is author of numerous books, including *Everything Belongs, Adam's Return, The Naked Now, Breathing Under Water, Falling Upward, Immortal Diamond,* and *Yes, And....*

CAC is home to the Rohr Institute where Fr. Richard is Academic Dean of the Living School for Action and Contemplation. Drawing upon Christianity's place within the Perennial Tradition, the Rohr Institute's mission is to produce compassionate and powerfully learned individuals who will work for positive change in the world based on awareness of our common union with God and all beings. Learn more about Fr. Richard and CAC at cac.org.